ANN CURTHOYS is an ARC Professorial Fellow at the University of Sydney. She was formerly Manning Clark Professor of History at the Australian National University and has taught at the University of Technology, Sydney, where she established a public history program. She is the author of many books on history, including *Freedom Ride: A Freedomrider Remembers* (2002) and, with Ann Genovese and Alexander Reilly, *Rights and Redemption: History, Law, and Indigenous People* (2008). She co-edited with Ann McGrath *Writing Histories: Imagination and Narration* (1999) and co-wrote with John Docker *Is History Fiction?* (2005).

ANN MCGRATH is the head of the History Program in the Research School of Social Sciences at the Australian National University. She has written numerous books and articles, including the co-authored *Creating a Nation* (1994), which won the Human Rights award for non-fiction. She also won the Inaugural W.K. Hancock prize, the John Barrett Prize and the NSW Women Writers' Prize. She has worked as a historian on public enquiries and commissions, has made television documentaries, curated museum exhibitions and developed pod-streaming history projects.

How to Write History that People Want to Read

Ann Curthoys
Professor of History, University of Sydney

Ann McGrath
Professor of History, Australian National University

palgrave
macmillan

First published 2009 in Australia by UNSW Press, this edition published 2011 by PALGRAVE MACMILLAN

Palgrave Macmillan in the UK is an imprint of Macmillan Publishers Limited, registered in England, company number 785998, of Houndmills, Basingstoke, Hampshire RG21 6XS.

Palgrave Macmillan in the US is a division of St Martin's Press LLC, 175 Fifth Avenue, New York, NY 10010.

Palgrave Macmillan is the global academic imprint of the above companies and has companies and representatives throughout the world.

Palgrave® and Macmillan® are registered trademarks in the United States, the United Kingdom, Europe and other countries.

ISBN 978–0–230–29038–9   paperback

This book is printed on paper suitable for recycling and made from fully managed and sustained forest sources. Logging, pulping and manufacturing processes are expected to conform to the environmental regulations of the country of origin.

A catalogue record for this book is available from the British Library.

A catalog record for this book is available from the Library of Congress.

10 9 8 7 6 5 4 3 2 1
20 19 18 17 16 15 14 13 12 11

Contents

Acknowledgments

Many people have helped us write this book.

We warmly thank the students in two PhD writing courses, one held in 1999 and the other in 2008. They were a pleasure to work with, and the ideas we discuss come very much from our engagements with them. The Australian National University generously funded both courses, the first one through the Centre for Cross Cultural Research and the second through the History Program in the Research School of Social Sciences, assisted by the School of Social Sciences in the Faculty of Arts.

Our publisher, Phillipa McGuinness, who put the idea in our heads in the first place, is much appreciated for offering many useful suggestions along the way, and for pushing us to get the writing finished on time. Our editor Anne Savage was not only efficient, but also encouraging. Graeme Davison and Alan Atkinson were extremely conscientious and helpful assessors of the manuscript, providing a mix of tough and useful advice. We also thank all those anonymous assessors and open critics of past efforts who have helped teach us about criticism and academic practice.

We are grateful to our audience at the 2009 Sydney Writer's Festival for lining up on a rainy day to hear what we had to say, thus reminding us how important history and historical writing is in so many people's lives.

Most of all we wish to thank Sari Braithwaite, our excellent research assistant, who worked on this project with great efficiency, speed and, above all, imagination.

Others who have helped us with ideas, discussion, or in the editorial process include Penny Russell, Peter Stanley, Spencer Leineweber, Christine Hansen, Ingereth Macfarlane, Lenore Coltheart, Barry Higman, Mary Pappin and Dave Johnston.

ANN CURTHOYS: I wish to thank my colleagues in the Writing Program at the University of Technology, Sydney, in the early 1990s for sharing with me their ideas about how to teach writing. Amanda Lohrey was particularly helpful in those very early stages of thinking about how to teach historical writing *as* writing.

I am especially grateful to John Docker. Together we taught 'Writing History' courses at the University of Technology and then at the Australian National University, during the 1990s, and from that teaching experience became interested in the literary character of history. After a joint residency at the Rockefeller Foundation Study and Conference Centre in Bellagio in 2001, we came away with a draft manuscript – which we later greatly altered – that became our book, *Is History Fiction?* (2005). Some of the thinking and writing which did not find its way into that book I have reworked for this one. John read drafts of many chapters and offered his usual valuable advice.

My new colleagues at the University of Sydney have provided a truly enjoyable and stimulating atmosphere in which to work. Bondi, my new home, with its wonderful, timeless beach has proved a real stimulus to developing ideas and writing about writing, and if it were possible to thank a place, I would.

Finally, I wish to thank Ann McGrath, for being such a good colleague and friend from our first writing workshop through to the final stages of writing this book.

ANN MCGRATH: Thanks for the thanks(!). I feel privileged to have Ann Curthoys as a collaborator: calm, reliable, understated, productive and wise, with a great sense of discipline, and a great sense of humour peppering the mix.

Those who inspired my passion for history writing, for which I am indebted to them, include Raymond Evans, Kay Saunders, John Hirst and Marian Quartly. I learnt a great deal from teaching public history with Graeme Davison. For insights into film and history, I am grateful to Andrew Pike; for art insights, my teacher Juliet Holmes à Court; and for legal insights, Mark Dreyfus and Hal Wootten.

I would also like to thank my colleagues at the Research School of Social Sciences, Australian National University – Desley Deacon, Tom Griffiths, Shino Konishi, Pat Jalland, Nicholas Brown, Melanie Nolan, Karen Smith, Daniel Stoljar, David Marsh and Tim Hatton – for their support for this project.

And finally: Milton Cameron, for patiently tolerating the extra work pressures; Naomi, who occasionally had to miss out on borrowing the car; and Venetia, for putting up with a grouchy mother who was trying to finish a manuscript at the same time as organise her 21st birthday. Not forgetting Sebastian the dog, who kindly offered walks among the wallabies in the Red Hill bushland of Canberra as a break from writing.

Introduction

NAVIGATING HISTORY
IN THE 21ST CENTURY

When Aboriginal elder Mary Pappin visits 'country', the dried-up salt lake called Lake Mungo in western New South Wales, she is walking over the remains of her ancestors and the remnants they left of their everyday activities. She talks about one of these people, Lady Mungo, as if she were an old aunty who died just yesterday. Lady Mungo lived here when the Neanderthals were hunting game in Europe. Walking this country, the historian can talk to Mary Pappin, and see the relics of the campfires that cooked freshwater mussels before the last Ice Age. History, modern and ancient, lies all around.

Historians are interested in the whole human past. We want to people that past with living, breathing individuals, as if they lived only yesterday, as if we had known them.

This book has some grand ambitions. We see it as a kind of GPS navigation tool for historians. You can take history's main streets, the wide highways, the back roads or the red dusty side tracks. That's up to you. What we have tried to do is lay out a map of the Country of History, and indicate the routes most likely to take you where your readers will follow. We provide practical advice drawn from years of writing history, and of teaching others how to write it. We want you historians – all of you interested in researching and writing histories – to be able to make better-informed choices as you write.

Sadly, historical writing has quite a bad reputation. Newspaper reviewers will often praise a history book because it's *not* like a history book. They will say it is 'as good as fiction' and thus 'a pleasure to read', or that they can imagine the film that might be made from it. It's as if historians have no style, unlike those cool 'creative' novelists. Historians also seem to have a reputation for lacking wit and humour – there's a lot of stuff out there about why historians are *not* funny, even a series of jokes pointing out how unfunny they are. As we write, a new Australian history quiz show is in preparation, involving historians – and comedians. The producers have paired each historian with a comedian, and pitted them against another historian/comedian pairing. Clearly, the historian has been cast as the 'straight guy' in each case – he or she can only be funny by accident.

We believe this reputation is unjustified. History, and historians, can be riveting, entertaining, and richly informative. Even funny. History can explain the world and place us in a better position to deal with the future. We know that history can live. Indeed, it can get up and do a tap dance. It can be a means of revelation – of the greatest stories about the world, of wonder and surprise at human foibles, of human achievement. It can reveal the complexity of that which we thought was simple, and clarify something we thought we would never be able to understand. It can transform our understandings and teach us to think from other perspectives – whether of culture, class, lifestyle or gender.

Some people think of history as just a jumble of facts, or perhaps a list of dates with events attached. Historians know differently; they love linking complex cultural and social contexts with the richness of the biographies of influential or ordinary individuals; they love to ponder how the historical legacies with which we are endowed were shaped.

It's possible that some might find historians a tad morbid. It is true that in a predominantly death-denying society, there we are, talking endlessly about the dead. But to us our daily practice does not seem at all morbid, for history is about somebody else's present time. It wasn't always the past. The people we research and their pasts come alive to us – we read their words, or words about them, we study their likenesses in paintings and photographs just as we look at living people. We hope to write about them as vividly as if they are with us in the room. We ponder the lives of those who preceded us, who helped make us, in some small way, who and what we are. So to us, history can indeed be creative; it can be poetic; it can be in Technicolour; and it can be three-dimensional.

Another good thing about history is that it's a profession where it's difficult to get old. For your whole career, people tend to call you a 'young historian' or one of the 'younger generation of historians'. So it's not an early burnout occupation. Indeed, age can be an advantage, for the older you are, the more decades of potential historical content you've lived through. On the other hand, there are plenty of younger historians. If you are a young historian, remember that your work can truly challenge the profession; you are the people who often ask the freshest, most intriguing questions – and from the perspective of your generation. You most easily embrace the full range of technologies and media for history writing, among them radio, television, the web, museum exhibitions. Irreverence is a great virtue of the young, and we need lots of it if we are to challenge accepted explanations for the past.

So, with all this elderly wisdom and youthful irreverence, why history's bad reputation? Critics accuse historians of being unable to capture the whimsical moments of the past, unable to do justice to the wonder, immensity, magnitude and excitement of our project. Journalists and popular writers accuse historians of writing only for each other. Noted American film-maker Ken Burns, who made the acclaimed documentary series *Civil War*, some years ago said he was trying to 'rescue history from the academy, which has done a terrific job in the last hundred years of murdering our history'.[1]

Yet some academic historians write wonderfully well, in clear, expansive and accessible prose, and much history does capture the imagination and inspire. Indeed, historians usually write better than academics in many other fields. Some books by academic historians have become bestsellers. Think of Annette Gordon-Reed's *The Hemingses of Monticello: An American Family*, which won the 2008 US National Book Award for non-fiction and the 2009 Pulitzer Prize for history, or Catherine Drew Gilpin Faust's *This Republic of Suffering: Death and the American Civil War*. Simon Schama's books nearly always sell extremely well, notably *Landscape and Memory* in 1995 and, most recently, *Rough Crossings: Britain, the Slaves and the American Revolution* (2006), which became the basis of a BBC documentary series and a stage play by Caryl Phillips. And there are plenty of other examples.

It *is* true, however, that academic historians rarely write the most *popular* histories. Popularity doesn't depend only on how well a text is written. Readers may shun histories that challenge their fundamental beliefs, or which are critical of their community or their country. Scholarly histories often examine the shameful as well as the proud moments, and can debunk popularly held and much-cherished myths. They may be confronting, or have unwelcome implications for action in the present. Furthermore, the ideas their writers present may be more complex and nuanced than many readers may wish to engage with.

Popular historians tend to be journalists and freelance writers. Most bestselling histories celebrate the achievements of nations, leaders or people fighting wars, and reinforce positive images and popular perceptions of people already seen as heroes. Popular historians often explore topics that others have already researched and written about extensively, and in synthesising in this way bring the story to a larger audience. Where there is original research, it most likely involves oral history, a well-accepted journalistic technique.

Whether you are writing academic or popular history, you need to write it well, to grab your reader's attention and sustain it. That's the purpose of this book – to help you reach the widest possible audience for your work. We do not claim to have the secret to writing historical bestsellers – although some of our books have sold very well as academic works, they have not, to our knowledge, been sold at airports.

Inside every historian, we think, is a popular communicator trying to get out. This book is for history writers of all kinds – whether student, freelance, academic, local, family, community, professional or commissioned, it is for you. It is not a book about how to be a historian, however. As a starting point, we are assuming you have some basic competence, interest or training – that you are already on the road to being 'a historian'. We aim to help your history writing get to a point where your intended audience will enjoy reading your work, and learn from it. We ask a number of questions: What issues do we need to think through in order to write more satisfying, more interesting, and more challenging history? How can we write better, more engaging, yet still professional histories? How do we write history for other historians, and how for a general audience? Can we do both at the same time, or should we write separately and differently for distinct audiences?

We emphasise the writing of historical narrative. Most historians agree that narrative is essential to history, but feel a little uncertain of how to actually write it. One of the reasons for this uncertainty is that in most historical training the emphasis is on argument, debate or the critique of another's work. What students are learning is worthwhile, but they don't learn how to write narrative.

Those who came before us

There has been advice on how to write history for almost as long as there has been history. The founding fathers of western-style history, Herodotus and Thucydides, who lived in the 5th century BCE, not only established what historical writing actually was, but also outlined their ideas about how it should be written. Much later, Lucian of Samosata, an Assyrian rhetorician and satirist who lived in the 2nd century CE, consolidated their ideas into a book of advice not unlike this one.[2] Lucian was very critical of the historians of his own era. After complaining at length about their bad writing, he set out his suggestions as to how historians *should* write, which included the following points:

- Focus on what is great and memorable.
- Be of independent spirit. Do not seek favours.
- Write clearly in a way the people can understand.
- Leave nothing obscure, avoid abstruse expressions and jargon. ('We wish the vulgar to comprehend.')
- Be just a touch poetic. Employ impressive and exalted tones.
- Make your brain a mirror, 'unclouded, bright, and true of surface' (then you will be able to 'reflect events as they presented themselves ... neither distorted, discoloured, nor variable').
- Brevity is always desirable.

- Give only brief descriptions of 'mountains, walls, rivers, and the like'.
- Be sparing with both praise and censure – 'historical characters are not prisoners on trial'.
- Write for eternity, not only for the present.

Most of this advice has worn remarkably well, and has been repeated in various forms ever since.

In modern times, advice about historical writing has generally been part of a discussion about whether history is truly an art or a science, a debate which arose with the drive toward 'scientific history' from the early 19th century, reaching its zenith around the end of that century and in the early decades of the next. Under the particular influence of the German historian Leopold von Ranke, a proponent of source-based history, the desire to see history as a science gained increasing acceptance as historians sought to claim objectivity for their methods and scientific validity for their findings. Many of the new scientific historians rejected the older tradition of a self-aware use of artistic language, holding the view that the historian must write plainly and purely, without artifice, as if there were nothing mediating between the past and the words they were using in the present to bring that past to the contemporary reader. This turning away from rhetoric, literature and an aesthetic conception of language tended to make historians unaware of the way they were writing, of the ways they could present their narrative and analysis, and of the various rhetorical means they could use to persuade readers of the validity of their explanations.

This narrowly scientific ideal, however, came under serious challenge from within the historians' own ranks. There were always those who emphasised the importance of the historical imagination and the arts of narration, scene setting and evocation. A number of leading English historians, in particular, refused to accept the notion of history as a science. Thomas Macaulay, author of the famous multi-volume *The History of England*, wrote in a dramatic, colourful, immediate style. In 1828 he castigated those historians who 'miserably neglect the art of narration, the art of interesting the affections and presenting pictures to the imagination'.[3] At the beginning of the 20th century his great-nephew, George Macaulay Trevelyan, argued very influentially that while the historian could discover the facts from the evidence, it required insight, intuition and imagination to give those facts meaning.[4] Almost three decades later, Herbert Butterfield, in his now classic book, *The Whig Interpretation of History* (1931), criticised historians who forget that historical writing is a creative act, which must involve imaginative sympathy to make the past intelligible to the present. The greatest sin in historical composition was, in his view, to pretend that 'the facts' were being allowed to 'speak for themselves'.[5]

In the decades since, most of those who have commented on historical writing have opposed the idea that history is a science.[6] The sharp criticisms of historians by philosophers of history in the 1960s – criticisms of the historians' typically weak explanations and forms of analysis, and of their tendency to imply causation without rigorously examining the relationship between events[7] – led to a flurry of articles and books of historical advice in the late 1960s and early 1970s. A number of historians responded to the philosophers by insisting that historians did have rigour in their work, but of a different kind from that we would expect in philosophy or natural science. Historians had their own modes of narration and analysis, and their own rules and protocols to guide their work.

This defence of historians' practices, however, especially their modes of narration, required some articulation of just what these practices were. Just as we learn a language without being linguists, historians had learnt how to write history without being able to specify their rules of composition and analysis. The American historian J.H. Hexter took up the challenge in an essay in 1967.[8] He argued that historical texts are different from both fictional and scientific works in that, like novelists, they will use connotative rather than precise denotative language and at the same time maintain their 'fidelity to the surviving records of the past', something novelists need not do.[9] In a similar spirit and on the other side of the Atlantic, British historian Arthur Marwick, in *The Nature of History* (1970), emphasised matters such as balancing chronology and analysis, how to deal with causation, explanation and description, and the question of moral judgment.[10]

The advice genre changed dramatically soon afterward, when the discipline of history encountered the challenges of postmodernism, in general terms an approach within the humanities that emphasises the impossibility of total social and historical knowledge, and the diversity and contingency of our understandings of the world. Postmodernism stressed the importance of the historian as narrator in his or her own texts, and suggested that we should be always self-conscious and self-reflexive about what we are doing, about how we are constructing our texts as history. Most notably, the American historian of ideas, Hayden White, popularised the idea that historians regularly and unwittingly use the techniques of fiction to narrate their accounts of the past.[11] He controversially argued that historians inevitably write a certain kind of fiction, and will furthermore write in a particular fictional genre, such as comedy or tragedy. White drew attention to historians' narrative strategies and techniques, their authorial attitude (for instance, irony), their use of plot and character, of voice and tone.

White's work offers an argument about the nature of historical truth that many historians dispute. We don't have to settle the argument here, and one can write history well from a variety of philosophical standpoints. But what we *do* think is important is the self-consciousness White suggests about the choices historians make as we write – choices about beginnings and endings, portrayals of individuals, scene setting, story lines. We are not novelists but we can sometimes think like them, drawing on the novelist's ability to choose from a variety of forms and work in one or more of a number of genres. We can rethink the ways we narrate the events and evoke the people of the past by taking on the novelist's concern with voice, point of view, plot and character.

The debates over postmodernism and history have influenced us, but we do not regard ourselves or our writing as defined by them. In offering the advice we do, we draw on our experiences in postcolonial, political, feminist, visual, cultural and social history and our work in different traditions of historical writing.

Advice on historical writing has traditionally been given by male historians, so it might come as a shock to suddenly encounter not just one female history advisor but two. Our advice is of course intended for historians of many kinds, on all subjects and periods, for men and women, young and old, and is drawn not only from our own research and teaching experiences but also from many glittering writers of history specialising in different eras and in various parts of the world.

Our aim is to bring together and share some of the knowledge we have gained about writing history – as readers and writers of history ourselves, and as PhD supervisors, readers for journals and publishers, and as graduate workshop leaders. Writing is a challenging vocation, and we don't claim that we always get it right. We have, however, gained some insights.

We were running a graduate workshop when we realised that no broad guides to writing history existed, and it was this which inspired us to write this book. Certainly there are books on how to write particular kinds of history – family, local, parish, village, company, oral and community history.[12] We have chosen to remain general in our approach in an attempt to be of use to all those kinds of historians, and to others as well. We hope our advice can assist the research student, the freelance historian, the specialist historical consultant and the academic. We hope it will enthuse you to write a new kind of history, and to write it well. We explain the strategies that you can choose to suit your project, your particular writing personality and your historical goals.

We have not written this book to model a history style. Because it is advising on how to do history, its style is informal and conversational – more like a seminar than a lecture, and not written in the same way as we would write history books. It contains reflections on our own writing and teaching experiences, and shares numerous examples from other historians. It contains many practical tips, all manner of advice about writing, and sections on 'do's and don'ts'. *Don't* follow us, for example, in using informal truncations like 'don't' and 'won't'.

We confess that writing this book enabled us to connect with inner gurus we didn't know we had. Perhaps unconsciously, we must have always yearned to write an advice manual – but not really known what to offer advice about. Not cooking, housework, gardening, relationships, child rearing, winning on the stock exchange or ageing gracefully. On writing history, however, we realised that we had advice to give, wisdom to impart, and people out there who may want to read it.

Like writing history, writing this book has been surprisingly exhilarating. We had a very tight deadline for the initial submission.

Perhaps it was the great speed at which we had to travel – with an eye on each other in our adjacent lanes – that gave us a peculiar kind of writerly adrenalin to reach the finish line. Adding to the excitement was the soapie-like suspense of awaiting the other's next dramatic instalment. Rather than labouring overlong on our words, and then bothering spouses and friends with grouchy behaviour, we could shoot drafts to each other for comment. Having someone eager for copy on the other end of the email was reassuring. Teamwork can be fun.

Even if you are working alone, writing history need not be a lonely and isolated activity. We encourage you to mix and talk to other people, to share your ideas and your writing with them, and to be interested in theirs. Learning about the past is, in the end, a collective activity, as we build on the work of those who went before us, and share with our peers, friends and colleagues the trials and struggles of our endeavours. Writing workshops, seminars and conferences are all useful venues for sharing ideas about history, and about writing, as we discuss in chapter 5.

For people to read, learn from and enjoy the history you write provides a wonderful reward. With that goal in mind, we start the historical voyage.

1

Which history to tell?

The good historian is like the giant of the fairy tale. He knows that wherever he catches the scent of human flesh, there his quarry lies.
MARC BLOCH, *THE HISTORIAN'S CRAFT*[1]

History writing begins with your choice of subject. You may start with a very hazy idea, so unformed that it's hard to explain it to your friends and colleagues. Slowly, it develops into something more definite, becoming at last a fully developed historical topic. You now have a program of action for your research and, in time, your writing. Choosing your subject is entirely up to you, but here are some issues to consider when you are at that very early stage, of selecting, developing, shaping, and refining your ideas.

It helps to remember the variety and ubiquity of history. History encompasses the entire human experience; there is no limit to its themes. The only limits to historical enquiry are, first, that the subject matter is located *in the past*, and second, that some kind of *evidence* survives from that past which enables us to know something about it. History can be narrative, descriptive or argumentative; it may focus on politics, war, social life, culture, economics, religion, ideas, sexuality or the body. The history you choose to research and write might cover a day, a year, a century, or a millennium and more. It might focus on a town, a suburb or a city. You might write a national history, or a transnational history that traces people, goods or ideas around the globe. Your history may be ambitious, attempting a broad sweep in both time and space, or it might focus on one person, one incident, one place. All these approaches can make for good, readable history.

When deciding what to write about, remember that you must *really* care about your topic, and there should be a reasonable chance that others will care about it too.

History that matters

Historians respect the past. As Greg Dening explains in the essay 'Reading to Write': 'There is a heavy obligation that I owe the past. If I claim to represent it – if I claim to re-present it – I owe it its own independence. Whatever happened in the past happened with its own uniqueness of time and space.'[2] In writing, reading and exploring history, you, like Dening, become steeped in historical time.

The present, however, is inescapable. As the Italian philosopher Benedetto Croce wrote in 1917, the documents and other survivals of the past are dead to us until we ask them a question, until we want to know something from them. '[O]nly an interest in the life of the present,' he wrote, 'can move one to investigate past fact.' A past deed or event 'must vibrate in the soul of the historian'.[3] There has to be, then, something in our present lives that sends us back to the past, looking for answers, looking for stories. And it's true, historical topics have always followed contemporary concerns. Natural and unnatural disasters – bushfires and floods, wars and recessions – often prompt new histories of similar events in the past. Heroic tales of exploration, great navigators and explorers, and sagas of democracy were ways of celebrating white imperialism and Empire in the first half of the 20th century. National history writing often follows nation-building campaigns, from the original formation of the nation through to national anniversaries and celebrations, or perhaps periods of national crisis. Economic history was popular after the Great Depression of the 1930s, and the global financial crisis of 2008–2009 may well see it become popular again. Increased interest in race history followed civil rights activism in the United States, and a rising interest in women's history came with new-wave feminism. Growing interest in Australian Aboriginal history followed the land rights movement. These days, with so many seriously concerned about climate change, more historians are turning to environmental history. As conflict continues around the globe, military and war histories flourish.

New subjects for historical investigation keep emerging, so be creative in thinking about what is a suitable subject for your study. Not so long ago, experiences like childbirth and sex, and emotions like fear and love, were thought to be timeless natural occurrences, without history; now they are seen as exciting historical subjects.[4]

Your own personal experiences will also influence your topic choices. We all come to history in different ways, usually a combination of the broader concerns of our own times, and our own particular life experiences. We, the authors of this book, are no exception.

Ann McGrath's story

Like any story about the past, the tale of how I came to be a historian is littered with circumstances, curiosity, passion and timing. I did History Honours because I got my best high school marks in History. My favourite part had been 'modern history' and I particularly liked the modules about revolutions, women's liberation, 'the permissive society' and changing the world. I was also very interested in any religion and culture other than my own (Catholic Anglo-Celtic Australian).The teacher who ignited my love of history recommended books of which my parents disapproved – and she was sacked from her job for it. As a rebellious teenager, history's thus-proven radical potential impressed me.

When I started at the University of Queensland in the 1970s, I enrolled in Asian Culture and Languages – but Japanese and Chinese required more work and talent than I could give them, and Asian history as it was then taught, focusing on politics and government, left me cold, although I loved 'Japanese thought and culture'. Australian political history did not appeal much, but when I enrolled in 'Australian social history' and 'Australian race relations', I was excited to realise that my own nation's history was cross-cultural, that it could open windows to understanding my own world. It seemed to have a potential to not only *expose* the hypocrisies and silences of the past, but to *make* changes: historical knowledge might be the start to sweeping away injustices.

My tutors, Ray Evans and Kay Saunders, then zealously exposing the horrors of Queensland's history of race exclusion and exploitation, became inspiring mentors. For me, their house was an exotic intellectual and activist milieu, connected to passionate scholarship from far afield. I was astonished to see the very latest imported books about race theory and history being regularly delivered to their doorstep.

Personally, I had some specific questions that needed answering. Why had I learnt nothing about what happened to the Aboriginal people who had lived in Queensland prior to the

Anglo-Celts? Why did Queenslanders hold such racist attitudes? Why were Chinese, Aborigines and Kanakas singled out for policies of exclusion and subject to continuing derogatory comments? In the late 19th century texts, parliamentary papers and minutes of meetings that I pulled from the university library shelves, the race talk was explicit and shocking. Someone needed to bring this out into the open. Historians had authority, I thought; they published in serious-looking journals and would be heard, but few had written on such topics.

In a historiography course, I read about the American historians of the 1960s 'New Left', and their desire to expose oppressive histories of racism and cruelty against slaves, and I realised the truly exciting transformative potential of history. If people knew about these atrocities in the past, I reasoned, the present generation would surely change their views. So I studied the story of the Asian indentured labourers who worked on Queensland sugar plantations in the nineteenth century. For my doctorate, I researched the story of Aboriginal people working in the cattle industry in the Northern Territory from 1911 to 1939.

Neither study turned out to be the clear-cut history of exploitation that I had anticipated. The Japanese labourers had effectively fought for their rights, and the Aboriginal labourers had made the cattle industry their own. Proud of their contribution, some Aboriginal informants saw me as a conduit to publicising their achievement; the tendency of many present-day Indigenous leaders to wear drover's hats as a badge of identity reveals that cowboy-stockman legacy.

There are still many lessons about labour relations, community benefit and culture that should be understood about that time, however. The stories of gender and sexual relations from these histories have a bearing on our contemporary nation that I still feel need to be further articulated.

The kind of history you research and write can be as close to or as distant from your own experience as you choose. Don't be afraid to write about something important to you personally. Many histories are prompted by a personal experience. Disability history, a growing field, is often written by people who have experienced caring for a disabled family member, or who themselves have a disability. Ann Curthoys has a friend who is hearing impaired and has written imaginatively about the history of deafness. You might write about the history of an occupation or industry in which you or a family member once worked, or perhaps still do; perhaps you grew up in a missionary family and you decide to write mission history. Some students veer away from such topics on the basis that they would not be 'objective'. In some cases it may be that you can't find a fair and balanced approach, and you would be better off writing about something else. More often, though, your personal experiences give you a passion for your subject and will help you write something truly meaningful and original. And of course these personal connections to your topic are simply a starting point. When you conduct your research into the past, you will inevitably need to investigate people, events and forms of experience that go way beyond the scope of your present-day life. It may be, for example, that your experience of racial discrimination has indirectly prompted your study of slavery, but it won't be long before you are deeply immersed in a world which is largely unfamiliar to you. You will be reading and learning about experiences that, given your culture, class and context, you cannot completely understand. But they happened, and you have some tools to help you maximise your understanding – a wealth of knowledge from a variety of disciplines, perhaps some useful theories and concepts, the work of other historians, and your own close reading of the sources. All history is like this, a mix of the known and the unknown, so don't be afraid to use your own experience and, also, be prepared to move well beyond it.

Once you have a preliminary idea, then it's important to see what others have already done. You don't want to embark on a major research project only to find someone else has already done it. It may be that you've hit on something that no-one has written about before, and if so, that's excellent. Even if someone *has* written on the topic before you, your idea may still be original. Perhaps there is an article or book on your topic, but it was written a long time ago and the author asked very different questions from those you are thinking of asking, or had very limited materials at his or her disposal, or it simply strikes you as poor or wrong-headed history. In these early stages, find all the existing histories on or near your topic that you can. In addition, try to find out whether anyone else is working on your topic. Ask around, and check out relevant conferences. If necessary, write to people who may know. (See chapter 10 for what to do if you find out very late that someone else is working on the same topic.) Once you are familiar with what has been done and what is currently underway you can shape your project until you come up with something that is new in subject matter, uses new sources and/or has a new approach.

At some stage you will probably need to write a research proposal. It might be an essay or thesis proposal or an application for research funding. While the requirements of particular universities and funding bodies vary, they usually include these common elements:

- Outline your topic and why you think it is important. Say why it matters.
- Explain the relevant aspects of your background, such as education, qualifications and previous publications.
- Show that you know what else has been written in the field, and establish that no-one has done exactly what you propose to do.
- Indicate the possible approaches to the topic, and what theoretical and methodological issues you will need to address.

- Outline your probable sources, written, visual and oral material, and show that you have some idea of where to look for and how to access them.
- Give a draft timetable for the project, including the various aspects or phases of the research, writing time, and revision time.

We discuss research plans in more detail in chapter 3.

A book proposal usually comes somewhat later in the process, when you have already conducted much of the research. It will be a little like the research proposal just outlined, but there will be much stronger emphasis on the structure and style of the book and its likely readership. Most publishers have guidelines for book proposals on their webpage.

Even if you don't need to write a research or book proposal – if, for example, you are writing a journal article or developing your own website – it is still a good idea to write a suitable and substantial proposal for your own private use. It helps to write down your thinking on all the above dot points, especially the list of existing works and the outline of probable sources. It takes a little while to check what sources might exist and be accessible, but it's well worth it. You might find there are too few relevant sources, in which case you may need to change or adapt your topic.

The proposal can also be one of the first entries in your **project journal.** Keep the journal through the project, jotting down ideas, references, leads and problems as you go. You'll find it useful when you finally start writing.

Ann Curthoys' story

I came to history through studying it at school. I just seemed to be good at it, much better than in my other subjects, except English. Very likely I was influenced by my mother who I'm sure, if she'd had a university education earlier in her life than she did, would have become a historian. After serving in World War II as a signaller for the Women's Auxiliary Australian Air Force, she became a full-time mother and an activist on the far left of Australian politics. She became fascinated by radical history and researched and wrote many articles for left-wing papers on people, usually women, and events important in Australian labour history. Her father had gained the University Medal in History at Sydney University in 1923, and later became a college lecturer in the subject. History seems to be in the blood. At Sydney University I studied British and American history, both of which fascinated me, with a very mixed bunch of teachers – all along the political spectrum. My honours thesis was on Rudyard Kipling's idea of Empire, but why I chose such a topic I cannot now recall.

Then I made a false move, taking up a PhD scholarship at Monash University. I knew no-one and had no topic. My supervisor suggested I study the Australian labour movement and the Empire, which I now think was rather a good suggestion, but at the time it did not interest me at all. It was 1967, at the beginning of a turn to a more independent, less British and less Empire focused approach to Australian history. It was also early days in the offering of PhDs at Australian universities; a more common trajectory was to study overseas, in Britain or perhaps North America. History departments had little experience of PhD students, and there were none of the support systems – the seminars, graduate coordinators, the writing groups – that there are now. Lonely, lost and depressed, after five weeks I decided it wouldn't work, and that I should withdraw. I remember telling my supervisor (a cold person who made no attempt to help me at any stage or to keep me as a candidate) that I was withdrawing, and fleeing to the women's rest room near the History Department, crying my eyes out. I returned to Sydney and began a Diploma of Education.

My story gets a little happier at this point. During my Dip Ed year, training to be a teacher of English and History, I chose as my essay topic in History Method the history of the White Australia policy. The main study in the field was over forty years old, and I realised there was a great deal more to learn. I wanted to know why Australians had been so opposed to non-white immigration for so long. This question was inspired in part by the debates then raging over sending troops in support of the American war in Vietnam. I felt that widespread popular support for the war was part of a long-held fear in Australia of Chinese invasion. It's important to remember that the war was justified as being necessary to prevent the Chinese taking over Vietnam, then swooping further south to Australia. So, when I had completed my Dip Ed, I enrolled in a PhD at Macquarie University. After the first year of studying racial ideas about Chinese, I broadened my topic to include racial ideas about Aboriginal people, and to see if there were any links between anti-Chinese and anti-Aboriginal feeling.

I've gone into many other fields of history since then – women's history, popular culture, public history, Cold War political history – but somehow those early concerns with race and racism, and with Empire, are still with me. It's been forty-three years since I began my PhD but I've never been bored. History still fascinates me.

Do we have the right to research and write any history we choose? Historians' right to explore all human conditions has been challenged by some indigenous and black scholars, who have classed outsider histories as attempts to speak on their behalf, that is, as 'historical ventriloquism'.[5] Their knowledge systems have long been undervalued by powerful elites, governments, economic and social forces, and these groups understandably do not want their history misappropriated in a like fashion. Around the world, a number of scholars are adopting an 'indigenist' approach to ensure that indigenous knowledge is drawn on for research and writing, and to ensure that 'intangible' heritage and cosmological frameworks and languages are valued and protected. In writing Native American history, for example, historians need to consider oral histories and narrative strategies so that they do not unwittingly undermine indigenous takes on history telling. Some groups prioritise language learning and oral history telling in their own language, to their own children; they value this over and above creating openly available published history.[6] They hold on to history as something truly their own, *for* their own. They know why they are doing it.

This doesn't mean there is no place for outsider histories. The best approach to writing history honestly and truthfully is to be able to scrutinise what you are doing and why *you* are doing it. A reflexive approach encourages you to be open about your identity and your aims in writing this history. You don't have to speak for insiders if you are not one. Don't lose sight of the purpose of your stories, your insights and your analysis. Remember that the history you write will be just one of many history channels that the reader can choose to switch on. But if you don't write it, there will be one less potentially valuable transmission.

2

Who is your history for?

*No other discipline has its portals so
wide open to the general public as history.*
JOHAN HUIZINGA, *MEN AND IDEAS*[1]

Having pondered what history you want to write about, and why, the
next question to ask yourself is, 'Who for?' This is perhaps the most
important question of all. If you can't establish who your readers
will be, you will find it extremely difficult to write well.

In this book, we want to help new and established historians write
history that people want to read. There is a catch, a trick, in our
title, however, as it all depends on who we mean by 'people'. Which
people? Do we really imagine our histories will be fascinating to
everyone? Highly unlikely. So, let's look closer at this desire to be read
and ask some tough questions. Do you want to write for historians,
history students, specific social groups (such as a community, a
family, members of a company or organisation) or the less easily
defined general educated readership? One of our key arguments is

that different audiences require different kinds of history – with specific writing challenges arising in each case.

Once you have achieved a sense of audience, you will know what kind of history you need to write. History has many houses – among them the school essay, the essay in a specialist journal, the article in a popular magazine, the PhD thesis, all manner of books. These different genres have distinct characteristics, though they do influence one another. Genres are not static or mutually exclusive; they always interact with each other – borrowing, reworking, fusing, transforming.

Therefore, the first step in writing a work of history is to be fully aware of the genre or genres within which you are writing, and their specific requirements and conventions. Then, while respecting those parameters and conventions, find ways to do something new. There is no point in trying to write a PhD thesis as if it were a novel, a professional journal article as if it were a textbook, a family history as if it were a legal submission or, in any of these cases, vice versa. However, there *is* a valid point in bringing into your writing something you have learned from one genre and adapting it to another. Even if some of the genres we discuss below do not apply to you, reading about what you are *not* writing may help illuminate the kind of history you *do* want to write.

Within each genre of history writing, there is plenty of room to move, to develop an individual style and approach. Some historians operate in a more scientific mode, being very matter of fact in their commentary or great quantifiers and statistics gatherers; some are overtly analytical and/or theoretical. Aiming for elegance and eloquence, others use lyrical metaphors and poetic effects. Many attempt rich narrative. Some go further to see their writing as performative, a style which demands scene setting, characterisation, drama, stylistic devices and powerful, emotive effects.

Undergraduate student essays

Most historians first learn to write history through the student essay, although some freelance writers of history – especially of community and local history and biography – learn by other means. There are many guides to writing history essays, and we won't attempt to duplicate their advice here.[2] To the students among our readers, let us say simply that teachers and lecturers do not usually expect your essays to produce original contributions to knowledge. Rather, they want an essay to demonstrate that you understand particular historical events, periods or debates, have the ability to organise and present information, can argue a case and offer a well-informed opinion. They also want you to demonstrate you know how to cite the work of others, to quote appropriately, and to produce appropriate footnotes and bibliographies. At advanced levels, you may be asked to write a 'research essay', which will involve locating and analysing some primary sources, and this can be a challenging and rewarding experience.

Primary and secondary sources

Historians usually divide their evidence into primary and secondary sources. 'Primary' refers to evidence from the actual period being studied. Historians see primary evidence as more direct, closer to the time and the truth. 'Secondary' sources are works about that period, usually written later, though sometimes only a very little later.

The line between the two can blur, and some sources can be primary in one context and secondary in another. For example, a history book is usually a secondary source – but if your topic is a study of historiographical problems or themes, then that same book becomes a primary source. Oral history sources are harder to classify. Although not from the time, they do function like primary sources in that they contain direct statements from a participant or observer.

Honours theses

An honours thesis forms a bridge between the undergraduate essay and the longer Masters or PhD thesis or dissertation. It is here that many of us first learn how to locate and use primary sources, and to do something original. In an honours thesis, you need to demonstrate your skills at engaging with secondary sources, locating primary sources, and in using them to write an analytical narrative. You need to fully reference your sources in a prescribed manner and compile a bibliography. Your main readers are probably two or three examiners. Some History departments keep all honours theses and researchers do sometimes consult them later on. Occasionally honours theses may lead to journal articles – but get the thesis done first.

PhD theses

It is in writing the doctoral dissertation that many of us first encounter one of the hardest parts of learning to write history – organising vast quantities of primary material into a readable narrative and a persuasive analysis. A thesis, especially at PhD level, is primarily a form of professional training, a means of learning how to and then demonstrating that you can undertake original research, make a genuine contribution to knowledge, relate your work to that of scholars who have preceded you, and present your results in a clear and comprehensible manner. The thesis is inherently a specialist work, with a precise focus. It requires not only presentation of research findings but also demonstration of your knowledge of the key technical aspects of the discipline: a thorough understanding of available relevant literature, and engagement with the ideas and approaches of other historians and scholars in related disciplines. You will have to show that you have mastered the arts of citation, quotation and footnoting, and can provide a relevant bibliography.

While you will present a PhD thesis to a very restricted audience – your supervisor and two or three examiners in your specialist field – this is not to say the writing style does not matter. For one thing, think of the examiners – they are readers, like anyone else, who will want to be informed and enlightened as they read. Your examiners may need less prompting or persuading than other people, for they are already keenly interested in your topic, but in most respects you need to keep them just as interested and intrigued as other people.

Both of us having examined a large number of PhD theses, we can tell you that we are always thankful when a thesis is well written, sometimes even exciting, with new information, ideas and arguments being put forward in an engaging way. A blow-by-blow account of what you have found in every bureaucratic letter in the archives is not the way to go. Nor is providing lengthy summaries of all your readings of other historians. Your examiners want to know what *you* have to add, what *you* have to say that's new. Indeed, they want to know what your thesis is. What is your argument? Your take on the topic? What, indeed, do you have to say? A mixture of evidence and analysis, colour, texture and liveliness will enhance readability and the examiners will be more likely to notice your key points.

There is another reason for writing a PhD thesis carefully and well. Many doctoral candidates go on to publish essays and articles drawing on aspects of their theses. The better written the initial thesis, the greater the chance that excellent essays can be developed from it. Ann Curthoys' thesis on the Australian race relations never became a book, but it remained a source she could plunder for years afterwards in writing a range of articles and chapters. Some graduates will be able to convert their thesis into a book, though that number is relatively low. Ann McGrath's thesis did become a book, and – says Ann Curthoys – a significant contribution to the field of Australian Aboriginal history.[3]

Specialist journal articles

Historians write articles in specialist history journals for other historians (including history students) in a particular field. There may be readers from other disciplines who are also interested in the subject matter, but they will generally be limited in number. Journal articles obey many of the same rules as the PhD thesis – location of the argument in its historiographical context, presentation of original research, full systems of referencing and citation. As for the thesis, the target audience is already interested in the topic, but if the article is turgidly written, even the most devoted fan of your subject will find it hard going. The main difference is, of course, that this is a shorter and much more focused work, and for that reason has particular structural and stylistic considerations. An article must establish its concerns and context quickly, and assert its argument strongly and concisely. It must present its new material in an organised and readable way.

It is much more important than you may think to write specialist journal articles well. Teachers use them frequently, reprinting them in course packs (or 'reading bricks') because they stand alone in a way the book chapter does not. They are much more likely also to be in electronic form than a book (though e-books are growing in number and range) and therefore easily accessible to an international audience. So write with not only your peers in mind but history students as well – numerically likely to be your main readers. Follow the conventions of the discipline, as mentioned above, but put extra effort into engaging the interest of the student, and strengthening that student's understanding and liking of history.

Some articles in specialist history journals can have a huge impact. The most frequently accessed article in *American Historical Review* online is Joan Wallach Scott's 1986 essay 'Gender: A Useful Category of Historical Analysis'.[4] There are many other influential essays; two that come easily to mind are Patrick Wolfe's 'Land, Labor, and Difference: Elementary Structures of Race', also in the *American Historical Review*, and Dipesh Chakrabarty's 1992 article in *Representatations*, 'Postcoloniality and the Artifice of History: Who Speaks for "Indian" Pasts?', in which he popularised the phrase 'provincialising Europe'.[5]

Serious books

US professor of English William Germano, an experienced publisher and editor of academic texts, has written a useful book called *Getting it Published: A Guide for Scholars and Anyone Else Serious about Serious Books*.[6] He outlines the way publishers classify the different kinds of books that academics, including historians, write – scholarly books, textbooks, reference books (such as dictionaries and companions) and trade books, written for the more general reader. There are very different considerations for each.

Scholarly books

A scholarly book, sometimes called a monograph, is written for specialist readers, that is, for other historians, including advanced history students at university level. It has the kind of historiographical and footnoting apparatus required in the PhD thesis, though perhaps not quite so much of it. Even academic publishers often ask historians to reduce their historiography, their footnotes and bibliography, for the sake of keeping the book from being too long and too expensive, and of maximising its potential readership. If you are writing a scholarly book, two main things to remember are that it must have substantial original research, and that it must have a strong overall argument and/or narrative. It must work as a whole, and genuinely add something new to what is already known.

Many history books started life as a PhD thesis, but the road between thesis and book is often long and stony. Publishers have quite rightly developed a dreadful allergy to PhD manuscripts, for in book form most sell very poorly. So do not bother to send your thesis to any publishers other than those who specialise in reproducing doctoral theses. Instead, send a book proposal. This can be based on your thesis, but the concept should be developed to appeal to a wider audience.[7] Even the scholarly book for a specialist audience has different requirements from the thesis. The audience will be broader (say 200 times the number of those who read your thesis), so the book must address the audience directly and have a very strong organising idea that makes it work as a book.

Textbooks

A textbook is notably much broader in scope than the specialist monograph, usually synthesising the findings of recent scholarship fairly generally to present them to a student audience. Textbooks are written directly for teaching purposes and with specific courses, or kinds of courses, in mind. The textbook will draw students' attention to existing work, and help them place that work in some kind of context; it will encourage them to search out and read specialist works in its field, and so become truly knowledgeable in the field themselves. It will tend to suggest further reading, rather than being extensively footnoted.

Textbooks can come under much more political scrutiny than other books, given their role in education, bringing special challenges for the historian.[8] If you are writing a textbook, you will be summarising and imparting a sense of both the traditional and the very latest in research. You will need to find an enticing narrative and colourful anecdotes. You will want to inform and engage your student readers, so clear presentation, informative quotes, exercises for learning and assessment, and good illustrations and diagrams are all important. The flavour, pitch and vocabulary used in a textbook will depend on the age level of the audience and the content of the school or university curriculum. Take note of these requirements before you start, and if possible, discuss your ideas early on with educators, who can also provide you with some examples of books that work well as texts.

Despite the constraints, textbooks can be rewarding to write, they are influential, and they *sell*.

Reference books

A reference book, usually in the form of a dictionary or companion or encyclopaedia, is generally a multi-author project, made up of essays or entries of varying lengths, from 5000 words down to 100 or 200 words. They do not require originality so much as they depend on the skills of choosing the appropriate scope for the entry, deep knowledge of the subject and clarity of exposition. Publishers of reference books often use them to promote their names; think of the Cambridge

Histories, the Oxford Dictionaries, the *Chicago Style Manual* or the Palgrave Companions. The compression required for a short reference entry has its own pleasures: you can write very incisively, and often there is room for witty or provocative judgment.

Reference books can be of many kinds: a national history, a specific event, a theme, and beyond. American scholar James Millar's edited *Encyclopedia of Russian History* is a typical example of the first. He introduces it as 'designed to help dispel the mystery of Russia', the first encyclopaedia in English to cover the whole of Russian history, from ancient times to the post-Soviet period. Millar outlines his audience. His book, he says, 'is not aimed primarily at specialists in the area but at general readers, students, and scholars who are curious about Russia, have historical events, dates, and persons they wish to explore or papers to write on the widely varying topics and individuals contained herein'.[9] Martin Evans, another US scholar, has edited a useful example of a companion to a specific historical event, the *Encyclopedia of the Boer War: 1899–1902*. This is an A–Z reference work with an introduction, maps, a chronology, reprinted original documents, a bibliography, index and illustrations.[10] Despite the huge amount of work involved, both editing and writing entries for reference books can be hugely rewarding, as you help to define and develop a given field for a wider audience.

Trade books

It can be sobering to realise which history books sell well, and which languish with few sales. As we mentioned in the Introduction, history books written by academics do not usually sell well, though there are exceptions. Many historians do, however, *aspire* to writing a book that will appeal to people other than historians and history students. If they succeed, such a book will sell many more copies, perhaps contribute to public debate and knowledge, and even make a difference to the way we live. We are writing here with the trade book very much in mind.

Popular history books generally share the following characteristics:

- They are narrative histories.
- Events are presented in chronological order.
- The writing style is non-academic.
- Most have illustrations.
- They usually have minimal endnotes and select bibliographies.
- They usually have a strong depiction of character.
- Many have a minimalist story telling style.
- They are often long books with short chapters.

If you decide to write a trade book, you will have to write in a different way than for any of the genres we've just discussed. Trade books have challenges of their own. While they may contain significant new research, you can make few assumptions about what your readers know. You should assume that they are intelligent but that they know little or nothing about your subject. When you look at the kinds of trade books historians write, you will find that they are usually written for well-educated readers, but not necessarily readers who are educated in history. As Germano puts it: 'Trade books are the ones most people – including you – read for pleasure and information.'[11]

In writing a trade book, historians generally become more aware than usual of questions of writing, structure and style as they seek consciously to attract the attention of non-specialist readers. You will need to pay particular attention to narrative, character, and emotion, discussed in detail in chapters 7 and 9. In addition to the project of lively story telling, two other main issues will confront you. One is how to refer to the work of other historians and, indeed, other scholars more generally; the other is the question of footnotes and referencing, for in these aspects the requirements of trade books differ from those of scholarly monographs and specialist journal articles. We discuss both issues at length in chapter 10. A less tangible concern for some academic historians is worrying about what their colleagues will think if they write something popular. We say that if the book is well researched and well written and has something important to say, ignore such thoughts.

Historical reports for a particular purpose

Some historians write for limited audiences or for special reasons. These histories are no less important than those we've just described; sometimes they have a huge impact in their particular arena. Here we mention just a few special-purpose histories.

Submissions for legal teams and the courts

Historians are sometimes commissioned to write historical reports for legal purposes, such as land claims and heritage reports, and for other reasons (e.g. Holocaust denialism, in countries where that is against the law). The formats of these reports are very different from those of scholarly or trade books, and arise from the particular requirements of the law. In reports for Aboriginal land claims, for example, there are increasingly specific requirements as to format, so stringent and unfamiliar that many historians find them difficult to meet while still retaining a sense of professionalism.

On the other hand, if you are writing a historical submission for use in the courts, you may be pleasantly surprised that large amounts of documents are supplied to you relatively quickly and easily. The difficulty lies in having to present your findings in a way useful to your legal team, which usually means being much more decisive in your interpretation of the evidence than you might like. The law tends to push historians toward a very conventional use of documents, and to rule out the more speculative (and exciting) aspects of their discipline. Reports of this kind do not need the historiographical discussion that PhD theses and scholarly monographs require, but they will need extensive reference to the primary documents. Perhaps the writing doesn't need to be as enticing as for the other forms we mention, but given that the aim of the report is to assist the legal process, it does need to be clear and persuasive.

We suggest you prepare yourself by reading about the experience of those historians who have written reports for legal purposes. Significantly, such writing demands a thick veneer of 'objectivity', so forget relativist angst and any temptation to throw in reflexive positionings of your authorial self, let alone any clues on who you voted for in the last election. In the adversarial system of the courts, they are looking to cut down 'bias'.[12]

Commissioned histories

A wide variety of organisations commission histories, very often to celebrate an anniversary. They may be companies, trade unions, schools or universities, government bodies such as local councils, or non-government groups. The people who write them are usually professional freelance historians who depend on commissions like these for their livelihoods, or academics writing in their spare time. They can take anything from a month to two years to complete, rarely longer.

Before undertaking any such commission, we advise you to contact your local professional historians' organisation and seek advice on tendering, rates, expectations and negotiating a contract. The problem with writing a commissioned history may be that you have to compromise the story you want to tell. If the commissioning body wants to see chapters as they are written, you may be able to deal with and perhaps resolve any difficulties at an early stage. Sometimes the commissioning body does not like what the historian discovers, and refuses to publish the result. To avert this risk, take heed of your contract; check whether you retain the right to publish your work after a certain period has elapsed, in case the commissioning body refuses to publish.[13]

Commissioned histories, however, need not be bland. One commissioned history that stands out for the passion of the author for his subject is *Fight for Freedom: The Story of the NAACP*, written by African American poet Langston Hughes. His postscript reads:

> I grew up with the NAACP, now in the second half-century of its existence as I am in mine. I learned to read with *The Crisis* on my grandmother's lap. The first movingly beautiful words I remember are those of the Bible and the editorials by Dr. Du Bois in *The Crisis*. My earliest memory of any book at all, except a school book, is *The Souls of Black Folk* by Du Bois. My mother, who worked for a time on Nick Child's *Topeka Plaindealer*, the Kansas Negro weekly, was an early member of the National Association for the Advancement of Colored People. I do not remember when my folks did not receive *The Crisis*. In Lawrence and Topeka and Kansas City I often heard them talking about the NAACP.[14]

Some writers must deal with highly charged issues. In Germany in 1997, Deutsche Bank appointed a historical commission to examine the bank's history in the Nazi period in relation to the taking of gold from the mouths and fingers of Jews in concentration camps. The question was: Did the Swiss and German bankers know where the gold was coming from? The Anglo-American historian Jonathan Steinberg, an expert on Nazi and Holocaust history, was commissioned as the writer. His introduction indicates the sensitivity of the issues:

> It is hard to be objective in such matters. Objectivity, if it resides anywhere, dwells in the free exchange of evidence and criticism. This report goes to the public in that spirit. It has been corrected and argued over by the members of the Historical Commission and the Historisches Institut, and that is as it should be. It now faces the criticism, correction and comment both of the scholarly community engaged in similar enterprises and of the wider public, and especially by those whose lives and sufferings were marked by this history. We have tried to tell the story as far as the evidence allows and we have tried to do so, irrespective of the corporate needs of the Deutsche Bank.[15]

While commissioned histories generally have different audiences and purposes from academic monographs, sometimes the two forms of history can be combined. One book notable for being both a commissioned history and published by a respected academic press is Robert Fitzgerald's *Rowntree and the Marketing Revolution, 1862–1969*, a well-researched history of a worldwide confectionery business.[16]

Family histories

People primarily write family histories about and for their own family. Many people seek to learn about their own heritage and to gain a sense of direct connection with past times. Such quests can take the researcher far from home, encountering many surprises along the way.

The possibility of finding a famous or infamous ancestor can spark great interest. Americans have long enjoyed discovering connections with the founding *Mayflower* arrivals. English people often yearn for a link to royalty or aristocracy. But fashions change. Australians wanted the same kinds of ancestors as the English until they became obsessed with finding a convict relative. In recent times, many Americans have yearned to find a Native American ancestor. And people from the New World nations have bothered many an Irish librarian about their ancestors.

Historical forces have often disrupted a sense of belonging to a certain place with discrete family connections. Many immigrant peoples and indigenous peoples have a special interest in learning about their ancestors. And the descendants of forced immigrants – slaves in the Americas and the Caribbean, and indentured labourers in other places – seek to know their lost origins. They want to explain what has happened to them and their families. Perhaps the quest for historical knowledge is a peculiarly human urge to retrieve ancestral memory. Children who have been adopted often crave connection with their biological parents, or at least to know something more about them. The effort many people put into family history, without any financial reward, certainly suggests that finding such information satisfies something within us. Perhaps it is a sense of displacement, of not having deep roots in the place we occupy, that drives such interest in genealogy.

Professional historians can sometimes be sceptical of family histories, seeing them as amateurish. Yet they too write histories of their own families. Sometimes these become crossover texts: in other words, reflective histories of their own family that achieve another historical purpose. American historian Richard White's *Remembering Ahanagran* explores his family's Irish history, and goes on to reflect on memory, story and historical narrative. Michael King, a New Zealand historian, wrote about his Scottish antecedents in *Being Pakeha Now*, combining family with national history in an interesting way. Using a family study as a focus, Timothy Kenslea traced the theme of courtship, engagement and marriage in *The Sedgwicks in Love.* Annette Gordon-Reed's *The Hemingses of Monticello* is a brilliant example of the study of an iconic family.[17]

Family histories are one of the most participatory forms of history writing we have. Many of you are likely to be writing a family history at some point, or be thinking about doing so. Try to make it as exciting and readable as you can. If your written history is valued by the family members themselves, you will have achieved your purpose. If it is written *really* well, it may also interest others, and that's a bonus.

Television and film scripts

Historical television programs and factual or documentary films come in many different forms and, depending on the target channel and time-slot, are designed for diverse audiences. Historical television has increased in popularity in recent years and now ranges from reality shows like *The Edwardian Country House* and *Who Do You Think You Are?* (in which celebrities search for the history of their family) through to documentaries like Rachel Perkins' *First Australians*. Some historical documentaries rely entirely on archival stills and footage, while others incorporate dramatic re-enactments, sets and settings, and visits to contemporary sites. However, television generally requires moving footage, and very powerful story telling is required to complement still images. So you'll need to think of the image almost before the story.

Television and film aim to elicit an emotional response from the viewer, so it is useful to create a structure with an emotional high point. If you are aiming at a prime time audience, you'll have to take account of what television people call the 'LCD' factor, or lowest common denominator. The big 'E' word is Entertainment, not Education, which is thought to put people off. Even the factually oriented Biography Channel and History Channel emphasise entertainment.

Historians can readily use their expertise to work as researchers in film and television. The technical side of writing scripts for film, and of constructing history by producing and directing films, is more complex. The scriptwriter, who must usually follow the director and executive producer's ideas for the program and prepare a preliminary script prior to filming, has to think through key themes, points and the ordering of events. When filming is complete, they must write another kind of script, drawing on a detailed log of filmed materials. A lot of the storytelling is brought together at the editing stage. Juxtapositions with other material are crucial: how the image fits with and interacts in creating meaning with the dialogue, sound, voice-over narrative if it's required, and music.

The historian can learn on the job by working with a team that is sympathetic to creating good history and patient with a newcomer to the industry. Alternatively, you might enrol in a practical film-making course. Or do both. A number of online advice websites provide sample scripts.

If you are interested in film as your medium for history telling, and want to ensure it is good history, you should try to create the situation where you can control various stages of production. This will not happen if you are a historical advisor, a role which can be rewarding but is restricted to providing factual evidence or analytical angles. Only if you learn how to be writer, director and producer will you have the same control over the history as you do in writing an academic article or a book.[18]

Radio

Unlike television, radio is a medium that can readily explore complex ideas as well as emotions and human impacts. It is therefore a great medium for history telling – and is much less expensive than television. Many historians we know enjoy listening to downloaded podcasts of history programs. Radio lends itself especially to the presentation of recent history, where living individuals are available to tell the story in their own words. Good editing can bring the story together and contextualise histories with impressive liveliness and depth. A range of history experts can be interviewed to explore different aspects of the story, to compare and contrast perspectives. Additionally, actors can present original texts with power and emotional impact. In radio, the full transmission of a significant history lecture still stands as a gratifying format. Radio allows much more scope than television for researching and exploring debates. Some historians also seek to turn their histories into factual plays that are based upon documentary evidence. Appropriate soundscapes and music, good quality voice recordings and good editing will all help.

As well as offering specialised history programs, radio news and current affairs programs are more likely to interview you and promote your historical work if it is newsworthy, or of special local interest. Don't be frightened about participating in a talkback session, even with a renowned shockjock. We have found that they are surprisingly well-behaved towards historians.

Brief articles for popular magazines and newspapers

When you get an idea for an article, especially an opinion piece, for a magazine or newspaper, the first thing to find out is whether the editor actually wants an article on this topic. Editors are conscious of balancing their stories, and of pleasing a wide audience. They focus on covering fresh topics. (You may need to pitch your story over the phone, as it's our experience that editors tend to ignore emails.) They want a 'hook' for a story on something topical, and often ask, 'What do you *want* to happen?' That is, what do you hope this article might achieve? Could it change a politician's mind about something? Politicians read opinion pieces, as do hundreds of thousands of others, so they can become a powerful forum for suggesting a change of policy. The piece needs to be succinct; it helps if there's humour, some witty lines or memorable metaphors. It needs to be snappy, lively and concise. An enticing beginning with a hook, and a thought-provoking ending with clear policy recommendations, are important, and the word limit you are given is usually final.

Such pieces require little or no historiography and no footnotes, although maybe an in-text bibliographical reference or two will be acceptable. What they do need is to be written clearly and well, to convey historical information and understanding to an audience that may not be especially interested in history per se, but which is interested now for some particular reason – a significant date, an anniversary, a 'day of' or, say, a new television series. The opinion piece has to be up to date in its thinking and approach, and speak very directly to the reader. It has to be informative, yet not too detailed. To beat other commentators and to be timely, the writer must generally be responding to something in the news the day before. This calls for quick finger-tapping, without time for deep research, and with little chance of editing your work. But do allow some time for fact-checking, and be careful about leaping to conclusions. You could end up reaching a million or so readers, a number of whom will be people who devote their lives to finding inaccuracies in anything they read. They get especially excited about tripping up anyone calling themselves a historian. There are a lot of wannabe historians out there and some are well read. Avoid the clanger.

Briefs for museum exhibitions

Exhibitions require a brief that lists the key aims, ideas, messages and, importantly, the objects to be displayed. The exhibition brief is a genre that requires specialist expertise and the abilities not only to write display caption text, but to work primarily with original and replica objects, photographic and art visuals, video and interactive digital media such as games and computer programs. Depending on the size of the museum or other institution, and the exhibition, you will usually be working in a team. One of the first issues is to consider how to develop your subject matter, then to locate the objects for display. You will need to seek permission from custodians and owners, who might be private collectors or public museums, a process that requires a surprisingly long lead time. Several months are necessary for negotiating permissions, insurance and transport. Professional conservators, registrars and others must be brought into the process.

With a museum display it is important not to see the text as the primary storytelling device. If you think you can tell the story through captions posted on a wall, you would be better off writing a book. Theme and content must be built up via the objects. The captions are important, but they are usually sparing – some museums specify fifty words or even less – and they must be extremely clear and balanced. Captions may need to go before many boards and committees before their wording is approved.

An exhibition benefits from being developed with professional museum designers. The historian may feel compromised working with designers, as the visuals start to dictate the story, and important details may have to be deleted to fit design criteria. Sometimes sound is used, along with artistic installations and special effects. Multimedia formats that seem to have expansive potential can, however, limit, if not constrict. You have to learn the limits and potential of each medium as you go. Don't imagine yourself as the sole author; you will have to get used to being part of the team and also accepting the decisions of an external body. (The same applies to working on many film projects.) As compensation for the loss of control, just think of the wider audience you will reach.

Briefs for websites

A website can reach a vast audience, and be valuable for presenting historical information in a multimedia and accessible way, although you need to be clear about its purpose. How do you want people to use this website? Websites can be designed for the broad public, a special interest group, particular community groups or invited users with password access. They can present history through public postings, discussion and chat sites, and information exchanges.

Websites are excellent for presenting visual and aural material – photographs, scans of old documents, oral history interviews, recorded voice and music – alongside your text. Design, content and permissions are important for web development projects. Analyse the historical websites you like, and think about how you could use what you've discovered to build up your own. Work with a web expert, taking advantage of previous experience in how best to design a site, the likely traps and pitfalls, the technical issues and requirements and the design aesthetics. New software programs are making it much easier to design a website, and experimentation will teach you a lot about what works and what doesn't. Image is as important as text, and pages too heavy in text will not be read. Poor layout will also make a page unusable. Try out your page on different screens, web programs and formats, and check that the hyperlinks actually work. If it is to be a live history site, you must ensure it is up to date on a regular basis. Before using digital archives and digital images, make sure you seek permission if it's required.

Digital databases are incredibly valuable for historians, and Dictionaries of Biography and other Reference Libraries are becoming increasingly interactive.

Chat-sites, blogs and other networking and posting sites will be increasingly used by historians for keeping up with the news, creating virtual access for conference participation, preliminary and post-conference discussions. Research surveys can also be hosted online via specially set up websites. Do-it-yourself websites like Wikis not only serve to call for and gather the evidence, they can also present it in both 'raw' documentary style and with deeper interpretation.

Podcasting and downloadable delivery

With interactive technologies developing apace, many more history formats are on offer. Television programs and radio programs can already be downloaded from the Internet as podcasts, but there is far more scope for historians to develop exciting new history delivery modes. A combination of GIS-linked maps, historical images, graphics, sound and film will provide historical interpretations of sites, landscapes and buildings. Think creatively, visually and aurally, for these new histories will be much more than 'talking books'. They will allow many choices as to how you would like to present history, and to have it delivered. It's up to historians to ensure we are at the cutting edge of e-research and e-learning formats. This will mean working to acquire some knowledge of technical capacity, working with technical experts, and devising modes of history design and delivery that use the full potential of the technology and of historical practice. Perhaps it will be such new technologies that will most dramatically change the way we think about and do history.

Whichever style of history you write, and whatever kind of readership you imagine, it's important to think about possible objections to your ideas, your interpretations, your accounts, and to ensure that you have put your case, told your story and made your argument as well as you can. Imagine a somewhat wary reader, someone you respect. Don't be frozen into muteness – set out to win such people over. Feel free to tell your readers something they don't know, or something that may go against their current way of thinking. Challenge them! They have bought or borrowed your book or article, or visited your museum exhibition or website, but you need to work hard to keep their attention, and you certainly cannot take them for granted.[19] The more exciting and alluring your writing, the better you can tell new stories, challenge myths and orthodoxies and, indeed, make new histories.

3

Crying in
the archives

*Historians immerse themselves in context; they give
themselves wholly and sensually to the mysterious,
alchemical power of archives.*
TOM GRIFFITHS, *SLICING THE SILENCE*[1]

Historical writing depends totally on the quality and nature of
your research. If you haven't done the research, the writing won't
happen, and in fact doesn't deserve to happen. You have nothing to
report. If your research has found a treasure trove of insights, your
writing needs to do it justice. Intensive, often time-consuming and
painstaking research is vital to history writing. Rich research leads
to glittering writing. Both deserve equal energy.

Research and writing are not strictly separate processes. Writers
of history rarely do all the research, and then all the writing, in that
order. Through writing, we usually process what we have discovered
in the archives and, as we write, both generate new questions and see
the holes in our research thus far. Only in the writing do we realise,
very often, just what our argument is, and indeed why something

happened the way it did. Writing sends us back to the archives, or to more interviews, or to the historic site, to fill in the gaps and to answer those new questions. We do not simply 'report' our findings; we need to turn them into what we call 'historical writing', which seeks a balance between reporting, analysis and storytelling. As historian Tom Griffiths has pointed out, historical writing is not merely the 'writing up' of findings.[2] The writing is as much part of the historical process as the research.

Many historians love the research so much they don't want to stop; they are happier finding information than analysing and writing it. Like a detective, the historian loves following a trail of evidence, with each thread revealing an unexpected twist or turn in the story. Unlike a detective, the historian often knows the ending. However, what the historian doesn't know until the research is completed are the factors that led up to the outcome, the sequence of events, the lived experience of being in that moment when it *was* the present.

Through our research, we become out-of-sync witnesses to experiences from times gone by. Words are fundamental to human communication: to conveying ideas, emotions, beliefs, everyday transactions, traumatic moments, incredible events, ordinary and extraordinary relationships, and personalities and behaviours. In research, the historian confronts many aspects of human endeavour and finds out about individual personalities.

Historians model themselves a little like judges in a courtroom; they value hearing as much direct first-hand observer's evidence as is possible, and from as many different perspectives as are available. Conflicting evidence, along with the published interpretations of other historians (if there are any), provides the basis for a well-informed viewpoint. In other words, it helps to get as much evidence, from a variety of sources and points of view, as is possible.

So, how to go about finding this evidence? In this chapter, we focus on written sources, the staple for most historians, and the places – the libraries, archives and private collections – in which you are likely to find them. In the next chapter we consider other sources, and some significant ethical issues.

Getting started

Sometimes it's hard to know where to start. Ann Curthoys remembers well the first day she went to the Mitchell Library in Sydney, part of the State Library of NSW and a major specialist library for Australian history, to undertake research for her PhD.

I had my PhD scholarship, and I'd worked out my topic, which was a study of racial thinking as expressed in the anti-Chinese campaigns and legislation of nineteenth-century New South Wales. I had read many of the relevant secondary sources while doing my Diploma of Education. My honours thesis had mainly involved reading Rudyard Kipling's stories and verse very closely, and the secondary sources about him. This was a very different project. It was time to do the primary research.

So, armed with my new writing pads and pens, at last a proper PhD student, I sat down in the lovely old Mitchell Library, with its big old wooden tables and book-lined walls – and thought, 'How do I start? What will I do now?' And I came to a full stop. I had absolutely no idea.

You don't have to be quite as clueless as the young Ann Curthoys when you start your research. We suggest getting started using the following:

- Secondary sources
- Subject searches in good library catalogues
- Other people's footnotes
- Google searches, including Google scholar searches
- Bibliographical guides
- Specialist reference guides
- Biographical dictionaries.

Read the secondary sources first. You looked at them while shaping your topic; now read them closely for ideas and clues. Scholarly footnotes form a kind of detective trail, telling you where trailblazing historians found the good stuff and, helpfully, the institutions that hold the best sources. Although you are starting off where another good historian has been, you will be able to go in different directions, and to follow your own lines of enquiry.

Next, search for all the other things in the list, in any order.

Google Scholar and other internet search engines are wonderful. They help you find all manner of references, to note ideas for further research, and to find out which sources are online and which are not. Wikipedia's range and ease of access is seductive, but use it with care, because it contains an enormous amount of unchecked material. In the early stages of a research project, Wikipedia entries can alert you to many useful issues and references to follow up. Numerous reliable websites, often hosted by universities or government organisations, contain chronological and biographical information and timelines of important sequences of events. Before you start your project in earnest, make sure you have your **key dates** correct. You can look for these in general histories and syntheses.

Companions and **encyclopaedias** can help you refine your topic and work out what research you need to do. For example, if you are new to North American history, you might consider perusing

Larousse's *Dictionary of North American History*; if you are seeking specialist insight into the frontier, try Lamar's *The New Encyclopedia of the American West*. For Native American materials, see de Loria and Salisbury's *Companion to American Indian History*. Comprehensive companions to national histories such as the Oxford Series, which includes the *Oxford Companion to United States History*, the *Oxford Companion to Australian History*, the *Oxford Companion to Black British History* and the *Oxford Companion to Military History*, among others, provide comprehensive introductions to significant historical topics, as well as useful bibliographical references.

Biographical dictionaries, especially those compiled by major dictionary centres, can save you much time and trouble in searching for key facts and dates. The *Australian Dictionary of Biography*, the *Dictionary of American Biography*, the *American National Biography*, the *Dictionary of New Zealand Biography* and the *Dictionary of National Biography* (Britain) are landmark volumes, many of which are now accessible online. Remember these are beginnings, not endpoints, and you should feel free to disagree with or dispute their interpretations, which from time to time may require revision in the light of new evidence and analysis. In such sources, however, the key facts are usually carefully cross-checked and fairly accurate.

Bibliographies are a wonderful tool. Check whether any are available on your theme, locale or period. Think of these as your friends – your historical 'navmen' or route finders. Search the Internet for digital bibliographies and linked archives.

Manuscript guides. Major libraries, or specialist libraries, are sometimes the only places that hold specialist manuscript guides to popular topics. Some are available in other major libraries, and increasingly they are being digitised and becoming available online, and in special digital archives hosted by major libraries. Being searchable electronically, digital guides are far superior to a hard copy.

Planning your research

Develop your research plan. (We give two examples later in this chapter.) Continually add to and update your list of the sources you will look at – in government archives, major public libraries, specialist collections, newspapers online and hard copy, and so on. Think about not only written sources but also all the other kinds of sources that may assist – visual sources, oral history, material culture, maps and the rest (we go into more detail about these in the next chapter). You will add to this list as you go on, and maybe, as your project develops, you will find that some sources you've listed will become irrelevant. However, having a list of sources early on is very helpful, and it's worth taking some time to develop it. Preliminary searches of appropriate record collections can also be helpful, giving you an idea of whether there is a little or a lot there, and how much time you will need to go through them.

You may be quite certain of your purpose, your aims and your research plan before you start but – don't be surprised – they will probably all change as you go along. For many historians, research is a journey of discovery. Preconceived ideas often end up in the trash. As disconcerting as it may be at first, you may have come up with a new understanding.

Be inventive. Think of new ways to get information. If you can't find what you are looking for, think of another way to get to it. Sometimes failing to find information is valuable – you can learn a lot from what is *not* there. Was evidence intentionally hidden or destroyed? Or considered inconsequential? Too everyday to keep? Or were certain voices omitted from public records as a result of the way they were created?

Your first interest may not end up being your final interest. Research *should* surprise. The past is never predictable, never quite as we might expect it. That doesn't mean throwing out your plans; it simply means you should be ready to revise them as you go.

Words recorded in writing

Historians rely largely on written texts for their sources. This is the strength of the discipline, but when its practitioners overlook other kinds of sources it can also be its weakness. Written sources appear in many different technologies, formats and kinds of collections. They are published and unpublished. They are written with quills, fountain pens, biros, typewriters, as carbon copies, printed by huge old printing presses or carved into giant wooden blocks.

So why have written texts been so important to historical research? Art can record stories, but not the actual words of historical characters. Song and dance can re-enact events, but not record them with precision. Complex language was humankind's great invention, and writing was the technology that first captured it. Whether in manuscript, typescript or published form, written words can survive time. In addition, they are often accessible, as public and private libraries, governments, companies and families have often sought to collect and preserve them. In their various forms, they are sometimes conserved because people have seen them as 'official' documents – or as precious for other reasons. Many countries have Archives Acts to protect government and other public documents. Specialist libraries keep all kinds of unpublished manuscripts and printed materials such as newspapers and pamphlets that others would throw out in everyday use. Published books and facsimiles of earlier books are also wonderful historical sources – and a copy usually survives somewhere. Now many of these are available digitally.

Historians generally love written sources. They are the closest we can usually get to the living human voice, and they can be powerful and revealing. Prior to the invention of tape recorders, movie and video cameras, writing was the only way to preserve words.

Useful written sources include newspapers, parliamentary and legal records. These texts are public utterances, designed for a crowd, or to please a police officer, a senior bureaucrat, the courts or a voter. They are fairly accessible, being available in major, specialist, parliamentary and law libraries. **Newspapers** can fill you in on the everyday, on key concerns, public knowledge and contemporary debates. Increasingly they are being digitised, making searching very easy compared with the old days of reading bulk collections that were rarely even indexed. **Parliamentary records** are full of a diverse variety of popular opinion, issues of concern, discussions about tackling major events and about changes going on in the world. They demonstrate democracy at work. **Legal documents** contain a wide variety of personal testimony, providing a window into both intimate and public spheres. Generally, their existence represents a crisis point – something departing from public acceptability, a kind of social correction or an example of social hierarchies busily undertaking the work of self-preservation.

Written texts may offer incredibly intimate insider perspectives. For example, a lover's courtship correspondence, the letter of a mother to her son during war. However, remember that **letters** followed conventions according to contemporary practices – in the early American Republic in the 1800s, for example, even the most intimate letter had to be circulated around large extended family groups. **Diaries** can be a source of intimate knowledge, too, although even the diary writer is communicating to some imagined audience.

Some written sources require a lot of work before we can ascertain what they mean. Archaeologists have discovered information recorded on stone tablets and on papyri in various sites, and the expertise required to translate them is mind-boggling. Hieroglyphs and unknown alphabets create enormous challenges. And earlier styles of handwriting can confuse the unwary. Before the 19th century, English used two different forms of 's', throwing out many a transcription – writers distinguished between an 's' at the end of a word, which they wrote just as we do, and an 's' in the middle of a word, which was elongated and looked very like a lowercase 'f'. Thus you find yourſelf reading documents that do not make much senſe.

Handwritten sources can be very difficult to decipher, especially those 19th century letters on flimsy paper where the author wrote first across the page and then turned it around and wrote at right angles ('crossing their lines'). Some written sources are in such a fragile state that we can only get access to a microfilm copy.

Interpreting the documents

Documents unite the historian with moments in the past; they can reveal its forgotten events, relations and relationships, ways of thinking and behaving. Critical use of documents is one of the staples of history teaching at undergraduate level, drawing on a tradition of several centuries, consolidated most notably by Leopold von Ranke in 19th century Germany, and since refined by subsequent generations.

In New Zealand, historians working on Maori land claims to the Waitangi Tribunal have had their work subjected to unusually tough scrutiny. Working at the intersection of western and non-western understandings of history, and in a politically contested terrain, they have had to think hard about what counts as evidence. Historian Alan Ward tells us that the Tribunal historians developed the following principles, and we think they are well worth remembering. In summary, they are:

- All evidence is of worth.
- No evidence is privileged in the sense it must be taken at face value; all is under scrutiny and tested against other evidence, as far as possible, for corroboration or substantiation.
- Evidence created during or close to the events concerned is generally more important than evidence created distantly from the event, though later disclosures can throw light on matters that may not have been clear to participants at the time.
- Parties to events often come away with different understandings of what took place, each set of beliefs being quite genuinely held.
- Parties to an event are always acting within particular cultural contexts.[3]

When considering the value of any document as historical evidence, ask yourself a few questions:

- Is the document authentic? Is it what it purports to be?
- Is the date of the document, if it gives one, believable or is it open to question?
- Is the document reliable?
- Who wrote it? Was it really written by the person who claims to have written it?
- Why was it written?
- Is it a first-hand report?
- Who was the intended reader?

You may need to judge each document by the context in which you find it – the library, court records, and so forth.

Understanding the language of the past

Remember that all texts are products of a particular culture at a particular time. As all historical evidence is encoded, you will need to think beyond the familiar shapes of lettering, to look behind the words or the objects. You should look for coded language, for distortions serving a purpose. You should find out as much as possible about the construction of each text, as well as about the wider culture and time in which it was created. The historian translates not only words, but also the values and etiquette of which they speak.

The archives can be both place of revelation and of obfuscations; the writer of the words you find on the paper may have sought to filter or obscure something, to disguise, to censor or to create propaganda in the interests of a certain group. The careful critique of a good historian will help prevent these guises working – at least for future generations. The historian scrutinises other sources and cross-references to find out what was *really* happening, not just what one source *says* was happening. Much writing attempts to hide the full truth, or at least to colour and mould it into a shape that suits an agenda – even if this is full of self-contradiction and confusion. Every text contains an inbuilt narrative, or two or three; a good historian deconstructs the texts and discovers new narratives, new potential insights.

Studying the history of a particular region often requires learning another language. If you don't have skills in the languages of the relevant sources, you may need to start learning them. Studying history only in translation can mean that you miss vital nuances and key evidence. Alternatively, you could collaborate with a language expert to assist with research and to translate texts for you. Depending on the period, an archaic language expert and/or a script expert may be required. This can apply as much to early English sources as to other languages.

You can't read yesterday's sources as if you were reading today's newspaper

The language of the past is a way of looking at the world, or a cosmology, that has now gone. Don't assume that you know what a word means just because the word is familiar to you. Even if your sources are in English, skills of translation, of crossing timezones and cultures are required as well. In late 18th century England, for example, the term 'interesting' did not mean merely something of interest, as we might use the word. It had a more active meaning, referring to someone or something literally *drawing* the viewer's interest in a magnetic, irresistible fashion.

Start with your online dictionary. The *Oxford English Dictionary*, with its rich store of examples of usage arranged through time, is online. To tease out more accurately what a word meant at a particular time, you might need to consult more specialised dictionaries. American, English and Australian dictionaries may differ not only in a word's spelling, but also in its etymology (word history). Language, like everything else used as historical evidence, is itself a historical artefact, and the definitions and meanings of various words have fascinating and distinct histories.

Don't think you can work out historical language intuitively. Historical texts present other languages, for they are set in a different time, in their 'own then country'. Don't assume that because a word is derogatory now that it was always so. Between then and now, neutral or even complimentary words may have taken on a negative tone due to specific events or manipulations. An early observer wrote down *gin* as the local word for an Aboriginal woman. One hundred years later colonists were using the term in a derogatory way that situated Aboriginal women outside the wider category of 'woman' – which could only be occupied by white women. Don't take a word at face value either. Look out for euphemisms and coded language designed to avoid self-incrimination. For example, Queensland's colonial police used the term *dispersal* on late 19th century frontiers when they meant 'clearing blacks out' with extreme violence, including killings.[4] Not quite the same as today's meaning of 'scattering'.

Evidence of **body language**, often reported in personal correspondence and memoirs, can provide subtle insights into human interactions. Read such accounts carefully, as the language of gesture has great historical specificity – and also differs according to class, culture and location. Physiognomic or physical languages are thus worth close observation. In genteel society in late 18th century England, a woman's blush was not a sign of embarrassment, but a socially valued proof of integrity, of truthfulness; it was a measure against artifice, a sign of the 'true heart'. Encounters between indigenous and non-indigenous peoples, for example frontiersmen, explorers, travellers and others, where there was no common spoken or written language, often relied on body language and gesture. In order to discern the meaning of gesture, the historian needs to acquire some cultural knowledge through anthropological insights, and must carefully filter contemporary interpretations and possible misinterpretations and mistranslations. Although careful reading of such evidence will often remain speculative, it can expand understandings and thus be enlightening.

Important types
of written sources

Let's look at some examples of searching for written evidence. The places you go will depend very much on the topic you choose.

Case Study One

You have decided to write about the history of the Sydney landscape up to 1803. What was this landscape like prior to the British arrival in 1788? How did it look? What flora and fauna were found amid its human landscapes? What was it like by 1803?

You have a range of good evidence from British perspectives of what the Sydney area looked like in 1788. The observations made in journals and diaries by officers for the first few years after the arrival of the first fleet of British ships are especially useful because these people were seeing an unfamiliar country and its inhabitants through fresh eyes. They were writing for a hungry European audience who wanted to 'see' what things were like in strange new worlds they were unlikely ever to visit. Less was said about the convicts, because they were just the regular no-gooders to be found in any London street. Details were given about encounters with novel plants, animals, landscapes and 'Indians' – as Aboriginal people were then called. The journals used the popular concepts of the time, popular books, ideas about 'mankind', the antipodes, and observations of indigenous peoples elsewhere. While the journal writers were witnessing novel sights, they were deeply influenced by contemporary ideas and assumptions. You need to find out a lot more about the shapers of their intellectual and social framework, their cosmology – the way they viewed the world at the time.

By 1803, the first colonial newspaper, the *Sydney Gazette*, was being published, revealing everyday events and interests in a world otherwise linked only by long, treacherous sea voyages.

Search the following records, circa 1803 – say 1788 to 1805. There is a wealth of material to explore.

PRIMARY

- First Fleet journals
- Convict records – archives
- Maritime traffic records – arrivals and departures
- British records – Colonial Office
- British Parliamentary Papers
- Court records
- Private letters – key specialist libraries
- Convict love tokens
- Newspapers
- Drawings, paintings, etchings
- Maps
- Built heritage
- Cemeteries
- Archaeological evidence
- Land surveys – of Bennelong Point, for example, to ascertain whether the geography was different before the construction of the Opera House.

SECONDARY

- General texts on landscape history studies
- General studies of Sydney landscapes and geographies
- Contemporary journal articles – scientific, historical
- Books – secondary analyses
- Theses – academic (an often forgotten source)
- Oral evidence? – Generally, for such a distant time, you cannot rely on oral history. Aboriginal descendants may still hold evidence from early Sydney, but the disruption and decimation of Aboriginal culture makes this less likely than elsewhere.

WHERE DO YOU GO?

- The state archives, newspaper archives, library catalogues,

museum inventories, museums, historical houses open to the public; art collections
- Bibliographies; digital directories of various kinds
- Places around Sydney Harbour; Sydney itself

Case Study Two

You have decided to write a study of the US town of Cornwall in Connecticut, covering the first quarter of the 19th century. The society of Cornwall at this time centred on church, family and agricultural activities, although there was plenty of room for dissent and unrest. Some of its residents were direct descendents of the Mayflower Puritans, and its families were connected with people who we now know became very influential such as church leader Lyman Beecher and his daughters. Much of the architecture, the look and original layout of this town are still intact. Although inward looking, the residents of Cornwall had a relationship with the wider world throughout the New England region, with major North American cities, and with the south. By the 1830s they were obtaining reports from relations living on missions in Hawaii.

YOU COULD RESEARCH THE FOLLOWING

- Published local histories from different periods
- Bibliographies of Cornwall and Connecticut
- Biographies of local people; scholarly studies of famous residents
- Family histories
- Church histories
- American Board of Foreign Missions
- Private correspondence (held in church collections, in universities around the country, other public and private and specialist libraries)
- Diaries and manuscripts

- Legal records relating to land title and town plans
- Legal records relating to court cases
- Church records
- Births and deaths registers
- Business records; agricultural histories and records
- Journal articles and books – regional and topic-specific
- Local newspapers and newspapers from surrounding neighbourhoods.

GO TO THE FOLLOWING PLACES

- Local historical societies – maps, articles, objects
- Museums in larger towns, e.g. New Haven, Hartford – look for pre-history, furniture, studies of lengthy timeframes, stories of vegetation, animal life
- Church libraries and specialist religion libraries, e.g. Yale Divinity Library, Sterling Library, Beinecke Library at Yale
- State and other archives; legal repositories
- Cornwall itself
- Chase up descendants; private family collections.

Digital sources and a changing research world

With the growth of the Internet and web-based sources, you can now access many historical and more recent texts in digital form.

Until very recently, because regional and national records were only available in repositories in their own states and countries, most primary source research meant the historian had to travel around the world. While newspapers and original manuscripts were sometimes available on microfilm or microfiche (both of which require special reading equipment and young eyes), most evidence was only available in its original form in a library or archive, and was rarely indexed.

In the 21st century, an immense amount of significant rare material is now available digitally. Genealogy sites such as Ancestry.com have digitised census records, births, death and marriage records, immigration records, and much else. It does, however, cost money to access, but a great deal less than national and overseas travel costs.

Adventures in libraries

Despite enthusiastic embrace of the digital revolution, there is still a long way to go. Most historical records remain in libraries and archives as physical entities. Early on in your planning, you need to identify the libraries, archival repositories and collections dealing with your subject – local, state, national or specialist – and check out their website catalogues. There are public libraries in major cities, and university libraries, and specialist libraries as well, some of them privately run. There's the Wellcome Library on the history of medicine in London, the Newberry in Chicago on early American and Native American history, the Huntington in California that specialises in the history of gardens, the Bodleian at Oxford on early English manuscripts, the Mitchell in Sydney on early navigators and the history of New South Wales, and the Marciana (St Marks) Library in Venice holding Renaissance manuscripts. Many of these libraries are housed in substantial, elegant buildings that make statements in themselves on the significance of books and learning. The Beinecke Library at Yale, with its white marble walls, seems to float on air. It holds a Gutenberg Bible, papyri and stone tablets. Other libraries are cathedral-like, full of neo-Gothic features or featuring stained glass domes. The British Library has just about everything, from some of the oldest and most significant manuscripts and books on earth, to the song lyrics that Beatle John Lennon scrawled in a café on his serviettes.

In these treasure-houses, you are now ready for an adventure. Once you have secured permission to enter, you can experience the pure joy of sitting in the peace and quiet of a library with a wonderful manuscript or a huge, beautifully produced, bound, engraved and illustrated book before you. Ann McGrath was thrilled to be sitting in the New York Public Library reading poetry in the hand of Dolly Madison – wife of one of the earliest US presidents and famed as a great hostess and role model for first ladies. At first disappointed when she found it was not Dolly's own poetry, Ann soon realised that Dolly had transcribed it to get her through her grief after her husband's death. Intimate moments with the long-dead famous, and many surprising close encounters abound.

The 'dry and dusty' cliché about historians only comes from people who have never experienced the excitement of libraries and archives. To a historian, the tactile encounter with surviving evidence pertaining to their subject of enquiry can be thrilling. Call us kinky, but if your passion is with the past, times spent in libraries and archives can be adventures of discovery. Living participants are as close as they will ever come to speaking to us directly, to helping us out with our questions. They can astonish and amaze us, and also raise new questions, developing our topic, throwing up intriguing puzzles that we previously did not realise needed answering.

The poignancy of some archives can also make us cry. Official state archives and historical society libraries can be places of powerful emotions. Relatives can become aware of shocking oppression or private tragedy suffered by their mothers or fathers; they can find the key to family omissions and mysteries. They can feel reunited with loved ones; for example, by seeing their grandfather's school report at the age of seven. Some people sell their houses and spend their life savings to travel the country to try to track down their ancestors. Others are seeking not ancestors but their own biological parents. Crying in the archives, joy and exhilaration in the archives, are all part of the experience of being there.

Libraries open the windows of the world. As you walk along the shelves looking for those relevant references and trying to match up the Dewey decimal numbers that appeared on the computer catalogue screen, you can stumble across other books calling out to be noticed. There is something magical about the way your eyes will light on something totally out of left field, and you suddenly recognise its possible relevance to your subject. Browsing shelves of periodicals and journals you've never heard of can also unearth fascinating articles (though these days people tend to do their journal searching digitally, which can bring its own surprising finds).

Ann McGrath

I tend to greedily pick such a huge mound of books – everything that might possibly be relevant – that it becomes an absolute test of biceps, elbows and balancing skills to make it to a desk without embarrassment. Others take the smarter option of sitting on the floor and reading in the aisles.

What is it that's so exciting about library research? Intellectual stimulation. Encounters with real people from the past. Forgotten sensibilities and insider perspectives. Archives give you the closest thing to a flashback anyone is likely to have – except perhaps Dr Who and other time travellers. It is these encounters with primary sources that make a historian an expert on a topic. There are no shortcuts from engaging with this material. The shortcuts are mainly in working out how you can find and access it.

Tips for avoiding library disasters

Getting access

Make sure you have permission to use the collections you want to see. Take lots of ID – driving licence, university ID, passport, social security number, letter of introduction from your university or supervisor; all of these might be called for. A first-time visitor to the much-loved New York Public Library, for example, has to get past serious security checks and then await the issue of an entry pass. Access to the Library of Congress and the National Archives in Washington DC is tighter again, requiring special photographs to be taken and what seems a top-level security clearance.

Getting there – on the right day

Work out your directions, the public transport timetable, and check out the opening hours in advance. A library located in a larger institution may not be open as often or as long as the building itself. Archives can be located in remote parts of town. Archival records take up a lot of prime CBD space, so there's been a tendency for some cash-strapped cities to relocate the repositories, or their storage sites, to cheaper sites.

Risk manage! You can arrive at the library only to discover that the file you want to see cannot be accessed until the next day. So contact the library and get some assistance before you turn up. Librarians' contact details are usually located on the websites. Many libraries are shut several days a week and some are run by volunteers of varying capability and training. Be prepared as well. After catching a train, connecting with two buses located at different bus depots, and then walking quite a distance, you don't want to discover that there is nowhere nearby to eat, so ask the right questions before you set out. Your bag will usually have to go in a locker, which often requires particular coins.

On another note, libraries are sometimes located in dangerous parts of town, so check this out. A colleague who specialises in Caribbean history arrived in Kingston, Jamaica and was heading for the archives. Halfway there, his cabdriver said that it might not be safe to go there. 'Yes, why?' The driver explained that the streets along the route were likely to be filled with rioters. If you have just flown into another country, it would be best to get up to date on local news before trotting off for more adventure than you may have counted on.

Obeying the rules

Every library and archival repository will have its own rules – and even cultural protocols. In one library Ann McGrath went to at Ann Arbor, Michigan a bell rang for morning tea and everyone walked out, including the librarians. Somewhat surprised, she continued to pencil notes furiously, only to be informed that the library *closed* for morning tea and she was expected to leave. Fortunately, she was invited to join the staff (morning tea was a huge box of doughnuts).

Even if you have to learn by experience, pay attention to the rules or you could be in strife. Because such libraries hold extremely rare and fragile materials, some rules are very, very strictly enforced. Sometimes you will have to sign privacy documents concerning use of information, or forms ensuring you will ask the institution for special permission before reproduction. For some items, you may have to request permission from the place of origin, even though a public repository holds the material. You may have to write to a church or other non-government organisation to explain your project and seek permission to inspect or publish their material. The use of names is sometimes restricted for privacy reasons. It is important that you comply with such requirements, as failure to do so could impact on the work of future researchers.

For conservation reasons, you sometimes won't get near the original, authentic manuscripts or very rare books, and will be given microfilm or a facsimile. If you have a legitimate reason to see the original, you can sometimes object. Surveying it for display purposes in a proposed exhibition, or wanting to publish an excerpt or illustration, may be acceptable reasons for viewing an original. Or perhaps you need to look at the ink, the cover, or see the illustrations in colour. Even then, you may need authorisation or be a specially invited Fellow to gain such privileges.

If and when you do get access to rare materials repositories, you will be required to wear gloves for handling fragile materials. You may have to place books carefully on foam or some other form of support to protect their spines. The library generally supplies the gloves and book props. Pens and biros are often banned; pencils and sharpeners may be supplied. Drinking water is often prohibited, as are coats, which have to be left in a cloakroom. This can be a problem when the weather is freezing. On the other hand, in the reading rooms of some rare books libraries, including the very warm Beinecke Library, putting a jacket or coat on the back of your chair is prohibited. If you wear it in, you have to leave it on. Bags have to be presented at entry and exit points; when you leave, they may be searched.

Getting on with rare books librarians and archivists

State, local history and many other archives can be very difficult to navigate. And that might just be finding the lifts and the toilets, let alone the books. Locating the relevant items often requires specialist advice.

At top research libraries, the librarians are very knowledgeable about the content of their collections, and may even be academic specialists in a particular field (known as 'manuscript' or 'specialist' librarians). It is always best to notify a library beforehand of your visit and arrange an appointment with the appropriate librarian. They can be extremely helpful, saving you time and directing you to material you might not otherwise find.

Remember, though, that most librarians and archivists are *not* historians. They can help you help yourself, but they can only provide guidance. They will not do the research work for you. They do not necessarily have a close knowledge of what their repository holds, for they are trained as records keepers, as generic librarians and archivists, not necessarily as specialists in a particular field. And although you may have travelled halfway round the world to get to a particular library, the librarian will not necessarily share your enthusiasms and have time to hear every detail of your subject. Professional historians may be in a hurry, and feel they have a high calling, but they will not necessarily get red carpet treatment.

Librarians and archivists see looking after the collection as their primary duty, not necessarily looking after the history researcher. Part of their job is akin to being a book security guard. Don't be surprised if you find yourself treated as a potential enemy/troublemaker. See it from their point of view. You are the disturber of order, the person who calls for the books to be ousted from their safe places, removed from their companions in their proper shelf order. You are a potential defacer, paper crumpler, page ripper, even thief. You are the one who could disobey myriad rules.

BAD MOVES

- Don't target the librarian as fair game to be your next best friend. Perhaps you are a long way from home, you've been reading primary sources all day, you're spaced out and you've got nobody to talk to. They are there to do a job and you are relying on them, so don't mess up the relationship.

- Don't even think of having your mobile phone turned on. That wild strumming, croaking frog or weird bird call will make you the enemy not only of the librarian, but possibly of everyone else in the room. And just think – these could be people worth knowing. In libraries are to be found famous writers, famous historians and equally famous ghosts.
- Don't rip the paper. Old paper crumbles very easily and old book spines are fragile.

GOOD MOVES
- Turn the pages carefully.
- Make sure you look up the catalogue carefully and transcribe absolutely every bit of the detail required. A letter missing, a number missing, and the librarian will have no chance of finding the item you need.

If you cannot get to a particular library, it may have a service whereby you can pay for a researcher to undertake some research on your behalf. For example, the Pennsylvania Historical Society, and various Irish city councils, can be helpful in this regard, and their fees are very reasonable. Interlibrary loans are often available, although they will be more difficult if you are after rare materials.

Research and note-taking, photocopying
The first rule of note-taking is to take down exact and full details of the source you are using. Never plan to make up for the lost information later; it will be much harder to find – if you can find it – and you'll be wasting valuable research time. Archives can be

tricky, as official files are often top-numbered and have been re-sorted over the years into master files. Go by the numbers on the outside file that you've been delivered. Make sure you get the full file number and the description. Then also note details of the letter, report, statement or other document that you are using. As you take your notes, also continuously note down the relevant page numbers or other details within a collection.

Most libraries permit laptops. Power points are not always readily accessible, however, especially in older buildings, so make sure your battery is fully charged. Using a laptop is probably the best way to take notes efficiently. Your notes are legible, and searchable. With internet access, you can search the library catalogue and the internet, to help you locate relevant material. Later, in the writing stage, you can easily search your notes to find relevant material, and you can paste direct quotes into your own text, reducing the chance of mistakes. Ensure, though, that your files are named carefully. Put the library and the collection in your title.

What do you take notes of? And how many notes? These are difficult questions. When books are readily available, you can have them by your side during the writing, but with rarer sources you need to extract what you want from them in the library, and your notes will have to be very reliable because they are providing your evidence. You really should write down much of what interests you, and much of what you consider relevant to your topic. If a document has only a few relevant points, it is easy to work out what to jot down.

When it is a really crucial document, it is often worth photographing or photocopying it, as you will find you need to keep going back to it and considering its meanings. Many libraries, however, restrict photocopying for conservation reasons. Because one library allows you to copy does not mean that the one down the road will. Many libraries will not permit copying of rare books and manuscripts, although some will inspect the texts you want copied and then determine the matter on a case-by-case basis. Be prepared to pay postage and to wait some weeks for using the in-house rather than do-it-yourself photocopying services. Even when photocopying is allowed, there are still traps for the unwary. You may need cash to do it, so bring a range of coins.

Increasingly, photographic and scanning services are available, making copying much easier and cheaper than it used to be. You can also scan and copy from microfilm, and the technology keeps improving.

If the library allows it, you can photograph the material, and this is a fast and effective way of copying what you need.

Our research assistant Sari Braithwaite explains

PREPARATION

- If you are buying a camera for the purpose of taking photographs of documents, ask the person in the camera store if you can get one with a 'text' setting; this will make the process much easier.
- I often see people with tripods set up in the library, but if you are taking photographs for research purposes, a tripod is usually not necessary. If you want to be very safe, though, tripods do eliminate camera shake and ensure high quality reproductions. Some institutions are hostile to tripods (the Australian War Memorial, for example); they are often seen as an health and safety risk.

TAKING PHOTOGRAPHS

- Don't use the flash – it blows out the image, and it's likely to get you in trouble with librarians and annoy other people.

- Also, have your camera on silent so the beeping doesn't drive the other researchers insane.
- Autofocus will generally be successful in picking up clear images.
- Hold the camera very, very still.
- If you are having trouble getting a good image, you may need to create a higher resolution image – so you need to fiddle with your camera settings.
- You don't have to get extremely close to the document to get a good reproduction. If you lean over the book with the camera, you're likely to find your shadow in the photo, which can look a bit creepy and also ruins the quality of the image. Don't worry about the table surface being visible – you can crop it out on the computer.
- If the document you are photographing is very thin, and text from the other side is bleeding through, put a sheet of white paper under it.

AFTER TAKING PHOTOGRAPHS

- Always, always check that the images are good reproductions before you return the material or leave the library. There are few things more irritating than going home to find your photos are blurry and unreadable.
- Every time you finish a task, upload your photos to your computer and flick through them.
- You need to figure out a digital archiving system that works for you. Label your images, and make sure you have all the appropriate references to identify what you have photographed.
- You can get software (Adobe Acrobat Professional, although it's expensive) that allows you to combine images into a single PDF. This is helpful if you have taken photographs

of large sections of a book, and don't want to review it one document at a time.

AND ALWAYS, ALWAYS MAKE SURE THAT YOUR IMAGES ARE BACKED UP.

Researchers used to hand-write notes. They put them on sortable cards and indexed them with alphabetical or thematic markers. Some still do. It works, though it's slower than using a laptop and/or camera. Recently Ann Curthoys spent three months in the National Library of Scotland where photography was not allowed, and she did not have a laptop. She wrote old-fashioned notes in three thick spiral-bound exercise books. It was a great experience, allowing lots of focus on what she was reading, with no worries about her laptop being stolen, plus she could sit in the less crowded areas of the library. The main drawbacks with hand-written notes are that it is slower than typing, it takes time to index the material, and it can't be searched the way keyed-in material can.

However you do it, note-taking is crucial to historical research. Don't just take notes, though – jot down any ideas that come to you along the way, in your project journal or another file. These ideas can be very individual, and perhaps not really relevant at the time, just anything that comes into your head in relation to your topic. You will find it very useful to read through these notes later on, and you might be surprised at how many good ideas are in there.

Endnotes and references

We discuss endnotes in chapter 10, but here it's worth mentioning what you need to record while researching, so that later on you can provide thoroughly professional endnotes.

With programs like EndNotes and free programs like Zotero, plus the digitised and standardised details of computer catalogues, referencing is so much easier than it used to be. EndNotes can save you time, and be a tremendous organisational tool. Ann Curthoys confesses to never having got the hang of EndNotes, though, and asked our research assistant, Sari Braithwaite to explain the program.

Sari explains

You begin EndNotes by opening a digital library. You have the ability to open unlimited libraries, which means that you can have separate databases for each of your projects, and different libraries for each of your chapters. Once you have set up your library, you begin the process of adding the references that are important to your project. The reference library will automatically organise them alphabetically.

There are a number of ways to add new references. The easiest and most foolproof way is to manually type the information in. You click 'New Reference' and select the type of reference it is (book, journal, newspaper etc) and fill out the relevant sections of the EndNotes form (author, year, title etc). A quicker way to obtain new references is to import, either from other EndNotes libraries, or from Internet sources. Importing requires a bit more technological skill, and it can be a bit fiddly, so you need to know what you're doing.

You can use EndNotes simply to gather the relevant bibliographic information, but it can also become a sophisticated database for your history project. For example, for a specific reference you can add information about the subject, keywords, your own personal notes, or the call number and location of the source. You can also attach PDFs to your references. Any words that have been entered into your database can be searched for.

When it comes time to create a bibliography, or add citations to your history, you simply insert or copy references from your EndNotes library into your document. When you are in Word, click on 'Tools' and click on 'Endnote' where there is the option to 'find citation(s)'. EndNotes can generate bibliographies and citations in specific styles. For example, you can export or copy your bibliography in the style used by the *Journal of American History*.

Many people seem to find EndNotes a bit daunting – but it is to your advantage to learn how to use this technology. Chances are, you are much more interested in writing your history than fiddling around with where the full stop sits. Through using EndNotes, you can save yourself hours of time.

I've had many interactions with teachers and students alike who tell horror stories of using EndNotes. But these bad experiences are usually a consequence of not being comfortable with the software, and trying something a bit too ambitious. If you're not convinced that you can learn how to use EndNotes on your own, there are plenty of training courses around. There are also a number of free online tutorials that you can refer to.

But always remember: back up your EndNotes library. There is nothing worse than losing your work to a computer glitch.

While EndNotes is an offline resource, Zotero is online and a free download that can be installed on any computer. The program was developed by the Center for History and New Media at George Mason University in Washington DC. As the amount of historical research material we find online grows, so does our need to collect and refer to it in its online form. Zotero senses the bibliographic information contained on a web page, so that when you click the Zotero icon the application gathers that information and places it in your library of sources. You can also use it to take a snapshot of the page and capture the full text of the online resource. You can organise material in folders, as well as attaching notes and tags to documents.

Above all, enjoy your research. Read or listen to or look at what interests you and whatever seems relevant to your topic. Discuss your topic with experts, who will give you more advice about where to look next. Tell your friends about what you are finding out, and see if they find it interesting. Don't forget to listen to them in turn and offer what help you can on their projects. You are joining a group of devoted researchers, so give others your time and interest as well as seeking help in your own research.

4

History in 3D

VISUAL, ORAL AND
MATERIAL SOURCES

*I went to visit my four sisters, carrying a tape
recorder and my imagined map of the family. It was
unsettling to learn that each sister has her own
quite individual map of that territory: the mountains
and rivers are in different places, the borders are
differently constituted and guarded, the history
and politics and justice system of the country are
different, according to who's talking.*

HELEN GARNER, *TRUE STORIES*[1]

In many societies history is kept alive in oral form, through ballads,
songs and stories. Some indigenous cultures have passed down oral
traditions that reveal geological events dating back over 10 000 years.
In many cultures and contexts the first histories were not written.
Biblical stories were first transmitted orally. Some of our best-known
written stories, including that of Robin Hode (Robin Hood), first
published in a broadsheet, were based on oral ballads. In Sicily,

storytellers travelled between towns, using painted illustrations and songs to enthral crowds with histories pleasing to the eye and ear. Indigenous people today – Native Americans, Indigenous Australians and many others – are proud of the songs, dances and ceremonial media through which they tell their histories.

The Oxford anthropologist E.B. Tylor reflected contemporary assumptions when he stated in 1881: 'The invention of writing was the great movement by which mankind rose from barbarism to civilization'.[2] It was presumed that only people with writing could have history and that only with writing could history be written. The study of ancient pre-literate or oral societies thus became known as 'prehistory', because of the lack of written records, though this term is now less commonly used. Historians thought that peoples who had not developed literacy in the usual sense, and therefore did not leave published records, stood outside 'history'. Some still think like that. Although most historians now understand the study of non-literate societies as legitimate history, they often leave detailed study to archaeologists and anthropologists.

Even in literate societies, written texts can be rare, forcing us to consider other kinds of evidence. Historians of ancient, medieval and early modern Europe, for example, regularly use all kinds of archaeological evidence – burials, architecture, ruins, coins, dinnerware, statues, ceramics, wall frescoes and sculpture – to tell the history of earlier peoples. Historians of domestic history use existing homes, and the furniture, layout, appliances and bric-a-brac within them. Unless you have studied archaeological practice, we don't encourage you to dig things out of the ground yourselves; an untrained practitioner can wreck the evidence, deleting a site's contextual material and destroying its integrity. However, you can research and help to interpret the materials that archaeologists find. As a historian, you need to respect the specialist techniques and skills of other disciplines and at the same time be keenly aware of how their findings can assist you.

Indigenous peoples around the world are today asserting the integrity of their cultures' oral histories. Recently developed cultural festivals often overtly celebrate and commemorate these histories. New generations of indigenous scholars are creating convergent histories that draw upon both western and indigenous knowledge systems. They are keen to keep not only the stories, but also the media for sharing these stories, available for future generations.[3]

Historians of any people and every era need to think carefully about all kinds of sources. In the 1950s and 1960s Fernand Braudel and the Annales School of historiographers led the way in urging historians to use every kind of evidence they could find, to become specialists in understanding everything relevant to their topic.[4] Among the non-written sources you should consider are conversations or recorded interviews with participants in an event, film, art, photographs, maps, music, song, monuments, landscape evidence, buildings, objects in private and public collections, and archaeological finds. Here we discuss a range of non-written forms of evidence.

Visual evidence

Photographs can be very powerful, seemingly immediate windows into times past. But given photography's relatively recent invention – in the 1840s – this applies only to fairly recent history. Photographs can create an illusion that you are staring directly into history: into a living person's eyes, into a living person's home. You can see how people looked, how they wore their hair, what their clothing and houses looked like, and who their friends were – information often not in the written archives. You can see their physical environment, see them living near rivers, operating boats, doing things. In photos you can sometimes sense the excitement of the moment: the frightened or cowering gaze, the exhilaration of flying pioneers at the brink of new technologies. You are seeing people also in everyday situations, in their work clothes or their Sunday best (though you should remember that they are possibly wearing clothing provided by a professional photographer's wardrobe department). These images are not like those provided by written words or speech. They are of the body.

We are not saying that visual windows into the past are transparent, or that a photo's two-dimensional framing is irrelevant. All photographs are taken for a specific purpose, according to a particular style or convention or genre, and we need to read and interpret them carefully. Many photographs are posed, so that people are sitting or standing or smiling in a way they do only for photographs, not in their normal life. Reading photographs requires special techniques; John Berger, Jane Lydon and Graham Clarke are examples of the many authors who provide further insights into critical approaches.[5] Don't overlook the rich photographic research collections held in major libraries and specialist visual repositories. Digital photographic libraries make large collections accessible from afar. Some libraries also specialise in visual collections, while museums and art galleries can hold revealing items of evidence.

Movie film footage, whether from a professional studio or home equipment, is another exciting way to see into both everyday and formal, official events. (Specialist film and sound archives house them, as well as other specialist libraries.) Ask many questions of your photographs and films: Why were these people wearing their hair this way, wearing this kind of clothing, why were they posed in this way, why are they gazing this way? How does the photographer shape the image, and how are the subjects and their gaze controlling it?

Some historians use **paintings** to gain insight into the past. Be careful here, though, because you need to understand the genre or style of the painting, the particular characteristics of the artist, and its purpose and context.[6] It is important to ask who commissioned the artwork, and whose tastes it was satisfying. Be aware of the modification of images in different formats over time. Always try to see the earliest version, as it will be closest to the historical moment you are researching. If you can study preliminary sketches, you may be able to follow the changing meanings of the art-based historical narrative. Later embellishments are also revealing of thoughts, attitudes and audiences.

Visual images are not just a valuable research tool. They will help you present your story and your argument when you come to write. They may be an important part of your eventual book, paper or website. So keep your research copies and notes carefully, in preparation for getting top-quality copies for reproduction in your published work. Take note of any permissions that will be needed to reproduce an image. We discuss illustrations in relation to writing in chapter 11, on preparing your manuscript for publication.

Objects

Objects link you with something used in the past and hence you, the onlooker, and the thing itself share a sense of connection with that past. Books, diaries, letters and other such 'word containers' are also things, but here we are concerned with 'material culture' – the historical evidence held in objects and environments other than written and visual texts.

Whether Benjamin Franklin's chair will teach you that much about the man depends on what you want to know, but at least it assists you in feeling amazed by your proximity to something intimately part of his everyday life. The chair enables you to connect with his surrounds, the surfaces with which he interacted. There is an excitement, an aura, a certain magic about connected things. Listen to people walking around a social history museum. Even the most ordinary 'old' domestic objects trigger memories from their own lives:

> 'Oh look! Aunty had a Sunbeam Mixmaster exactly the same as this one!'
> 'Oh yes, I remember baking scones in those trays and covering them with molasses during the war!'
> 'Remember old Uncle Milton and how he'd sit next to his big wireless in the den?'

Oral histories may be required to make sense of 'things' and their articulation in everyday life.

Human beings respond in complex, sensate ways to three-dimensional objects. We imbue the objects we encounter with meaning; the power of these associations can be readily observed in the concept of 'destination objects' displayed in museums. An item associated with a famous person – such as bushranger Ned Kelly's armour, Captain Cook's telescope, Galileo's Bible, Charles Darwin's marital ruminations or Leonardo da Vinci's paints – evokes tangible links with significant events. Visitors to Trinity College Library in Dublin line up to see the Book of Kells. When it arrived in Australia, people camped in carparks and waited in long lines to engage with this iconic object that has survived a tumultuous past. Sometimes the perilous story of an object's protection and preservation is as intriguing as the thing itself. The travelling exhibition *A Day in Pompeii*, featuring once ordinary household items, attracted record crowds of all ages. Objects can symbolise momentous stories, signify important moments of history and play a role in identity narratives. Devout Christians went to great trouble to obtain relics of the saints, which were sometimes actual human remains. Many historical objects become 'secular relics', worshipped as evoking histories, heritages, nostalgia.[7]

Ann McGrath

At the National Museum of Australia I saw the dress worn by Azaria Chamberlain, the baby allegedly taken by a dingo at Ayers Rock in Central Australia in the 1980s, whose mother Lindy was subsequently jailed for her murder.

My direct encounter with the object seemed proof of how authentic things could unsettle historical perceptions – seeing this dress certainly disturbed my preconception that Lindy was guilty. That the dress was black had led to popular speculation about the mother having sacrificed the missing baby in the desert. But when I actually saw it, I was struck by its message of maternal tenderness and felt moved and connected to it. I thought, *Her mother made this gorgeous little dress – with its lace hem delicately trimmed with red satin ribbon. How lovely.* I was also aware that black had been a fashionable colour for infants in the Victorian era, so it was not indelibly evil to dress your baby this way. Lindy Chamberlain's bad name had come about partly because she did not dress her baby in the current baby-pastel fashion.

While I was still standing in front of the display case, a middle-aged woman and her younger companion were also drawn to the tiny dress. I overheard their comments: 'Look at that! Shocking! Dressing a baby in black! What a dreadful mother. Well that *proves* she did it.' And the two walked off. Vindicated, satisfied to see the 'proof' – not challenged in the least.

Like texts, objects can say different things to different onlookers. We need to think a little differently to learn what an object has to say. Like all historical evidence, an object must be viewed in as rich and as detailed a historical context as possible – as in the case of Ned Kelly's helmet, where X-ray tests provided additional clues that revealed some of the mysteries of its manufacture and use. Archaeologists working on stone tools, for example, often experiment with making their own and testing how well they work. If we historians are serious about learning from objects, we should perhaps become more practical and apply some techniques from other disciplines. Close observance can discern wear-patterns. Ann McGrath studied children's cowboy and Indians outfits from the 1960s, investigating the symbolism of their hybrid Hollywood motifs. The wear patterns of the garments, combined with complementary evidence such as home videos and oral reminiscence, showed how these dress-up fashions provided, particularly for girls, an empowering outer layer when worn over ordinary clothing.[8]

A stout pair of boots

When historians visit the sites where historical events occurred, taking notes and photographs, what can they learn from their field trips? Michael Cathcart quipped that he was on a quest for adjectives.[9] Perhaps we *are* looking for colourful ways to describe a place, and the experience of being in that place, in a way that can only be gained by being there. Often, without having actually seen it with our own eyes, we can feel we don't have the authority to imaginatively 'be there' and thus share that experience. It's as if we owe our readers the trouble of going there. Whether you are studying the North Pole,

Antarctica or the Gobi Desert, going there may provide you with a particular connection with place.

In an influential radio lecture in 1976, the well-known Australian historian Manning Clark was insistent about field trips. He urged historians to always visit the location where the events they are describing took place. He quoted R.H. Tawney, the British economic historian, as saying a historian needed a good pair of boots, and added that the intrepid historian also needs a notebook and a pen, to write down the thoughts that come to mind when 'in the presence of some mighty spirit from the past'. Place, Clark thought, sparks a moment of understanding, of illumination.[10] Responses to place can provide not only analytical insights but also a more 'romantic' engagement with the place being researched.

'Stout boots' may sound as though the historian is a man striding out into the wilderness, or the battlefield, seeking historical information and understanding. They also evoke the tradition of 'slummer journalism', or social exploration, pioneered in the 19th century, where the observer would explore the hidden secret parts of the city, and write about life in the urban underworld.[11]

Whatever images and references come to mind at the mention of a stout pair of boots, we agree that going to the places where your historical actors lived, worked and played enhances most history writing, and for some kinds of history it is essential. Sadly but realistically, women may need to visit some places in pairs or groups – but, wherever practicable and affordable, go they must.

Ann McGrath

When as a young woman undertaking research in some outback towns in 1978 for my PhD on the pre-World War II cattle industry,

I discovered that the only place to stay was the local pub, and the only other females nearby were camels. I became wary when helpful males warned me of the 'danger' of going back to my room unaccompanied (by them). I adopted an exaggerated, over-confident gait, assuring them that they needed another beer as a nightcap. Before retiring, however, in a dodgy room with see-through plastic curtains, I devised a way of pushing the wardrobe against the door, assuring myself of a less anxious night.

Environmental historians, especially, stress the importance of seeing the places and landscapes they discuss, even if, or perhaps especially if, these places have been transformed since the time they are writing about. Military historians, too, need to see the sites of battles to understand their documentary evidence. Women's history specialists can gain understanding from seeing the domestic interiors in which women lived and worked, and the public spaces from which they were so often excluded and for entry into which some fought so hard.

In fact, all kinds of historians can learn by going to a place. Iain McCalman talks about how he gained insight into the life of the young British naturalist Alfred Russel Wallace, who in 1846 slept overnight in a vast limestone cave in south Wales with his brother. They could have stayed in an inn, but preferred the cave as part of their preparation for future travels and adventures. To research his book *Darwin's Armada: How Four Voyagers to Australasia Won the Battle for Evolution and Changed the World*, Iain lay down on the same cold stones. He said:

I lay down on the boulders and I thought, 'Christ! How could you do this? ... It was just really, really uncomfortable and it was freezing cold, even though I was there in daylight. But suddenly I got the sense of what a strange thing [it was] – these two working-class boys in Wales, with no education, who think, 'I'm going to go to the Amazon', and the best way to test yourself is follow this stream and lie on a stone in a cave in Wales. They were excited kids on an amazing, dangerous adventure.[12]

We learn not only about the site of events long ago, but also about how, or if, that event is remembered today.

Ann Curthoys

I visited the NSW township of Young, near the site of the anti-Chinese riots of 1861, for my doctoral research on responses to Chinese immigration. There I saw not only the uneven terrain of the goldfields but also the local historical museum, which displayed the flag of the anti-Chinese European miners: 'Roll Up, Roll Up, No Chinese'. I had read of the flag in the colonial newspapers, but to actually see it helped me gain a real sense of these men – often from politically restive backgrounds in Britain – using their political protest skills against the Chinese miners in their midst. That it was still in a country museum also told me something about how the riots were remembered.

Yet we need to be careful when using present sites to understand the past. They may have changed in important ways – the course of a river has been altered, a beach may be hundreds of metres from its 1820s location, a swamp may have been reclaimed, a hillside levelled, a bridge collapsed, and so on. What looks treed and beautiful now may have been dusty and ugly then, and vice versa.

Oral histories

Recorded oral histories are a major resource for the historian of more recent times. As most of us realise, however, you need to use oral history with understanding and care. Particularly since the 1970s, those of us working in oral history have been preoccupied with the problem of the nature and reliability of memory. Luisa Passerini argued in the late 1970s that the silences, discrepancies and inconsistencies that she encountered in her interviews with Italian workers about the Fascist period from 1922 to 1943 were themselves forms of culture that historians needed to understand. The oral sources were indications of subjectivity, of feelings and ideas about the past seen through the lens of the present.[13] In the 1990s Italian historian Alessandro Portelli also suggested that factual errors were worthy of serious consideration. He found that the people he interviewed in a small working-class Italian city about events that occurred twenty years or so earlier misremembered events in systematic and revealing ways.[14]

With these ideas in mind, historians came to study oral history mainly as a form of memory – more important for revealing ways people narrate the past and make meaning than as a set of clues about the past. To understand the meaning of the stories people tell them, historians have had to investigate not only questions of subjectivity, the self and identity, but also the building blocks of storytelling – rhetoric, metaphor and narration. While Portelli himself suggests oral history should serve as both a source of information about the past and a site of cultural study in itself, many in the field have ceased to see oral history as evidence about the past at all, but only as evidence about the present. That is, they interpret oral history interviews anthropologically, but not historically.

We sympathise with this emphasis on understanding memory. But we also think oral history can provide clues to the past, just as written sources do. Neither can be used naively; both can add insight and information.

Used wisely, oral histories can confront you with the lived experience and its longer term legacies; they can reconfigure your narrative by reframing the story according to a different logic and plot line from your own. They can bring knowledge of the everyday that is not recorded anywhere else. Oral histories of daily working lives, of routines and patterns of play and leisure, can reveal hidden histories. Many stories can only be learnt via oral histories: of a soldier fighting in a war, of a family escaping over a forbidden border at peril of violent death, of the near-fatal boat-trips of refugees on their journey toward a new life.

Oral history does have its particular pitfalls, though. If you are using oral history evidence, pay close attention to cross-checking factual information, because memory is indeed often unreliable on exact detail. The benefit of using these materials is the sharing of recollections of a lived past, but the reconstructions over time, the previous retellings, converged stories, and the tendency to judge the past through the spectrum of the present can also blur that past.

Historians use two main kinds of oral history – the interviews completed by others, in some cases several decades earlier, and those they conduct for their own projects. Recorded oral histories are available in special library and local history collections. Search for them and, if possible, listen to the tapes rather than just reading transcriptions. Much of the meaning and the authenticity of the voice can be lost in transcript. Where the written form is available digitally, you will be able to search more effectively than via content guides and catalogue entries.

Interviewing

You won't always be lucky enough to find pre-existing recordings of your chosen subject and you may need to conduct interviews of your own. You can interview using just audio equipment, or using video or film. Your choice of sound alone, or sound and vision, really depends on the topic, the relationship you need to build, your funding, and how you are going to present your finished history. The advantage of film is being able to record information such as facial expressions and body language, and the location of the interview. You may also be able to use the filmed interview on a website, or later in a documentary film. On the other hand, filming is more intrusive and less like a regular conversation. That said, many people, despite initial protests, adapt quickly and become quite at ease. The following advice applies to both audio and filmed interviews.

Before you set about interviewing, have a look at some of the books and guides available to assist you,[15] and note that you may need to get ethical clearance from your university or other institution. Oral history has its own set of ethical issues. Over time, oral historians have come to agree on the following principles and practices:

- Inform interviewees of the nature and aims of the project for which you are conducting the interviews in terms that are clear and meaningful to them.
- Gain the (informed) written consent of interviewees before recording, transcribing, or quoting them in your work.
- Give interviewees the opportunity to amend any quotations that will be attributed to them.
- Gain the interviewee's consent before you place the recordings and/or transcripts in a public library. It is usually best to make this consent part of the original consent form signed at the time of interview.

- Avoid disturbing or upsetting those you interview. Talking about the past stirs up both welcome and unwelcome memories, and the experience may be distressing. Sometimes, though, it is highly therapeutic. You should be prepared for these varying responses, and act always with consideration towards your interviewees.

Choose your technology carefully; digital recorders and voice recognition software may be worth using. You have to be practical and check that your equipment is all working well, and ensure that you are confident about using it. Nervousness on your part will only make your interviewee uncomfortable. The saddest research tales are about wonderful interviews that ended up being blank tapes because the historian pressed the wrong button.

Contact your potential interviewee by mail or by phone. Many people are nervous about the idea of being recorded by someone they don't know, although you will find that older people are often keen to share their histories and thoroughly enjoy the experience of their story being valued by someone else. Be very clear about the general topic you wish to cover. Tell them about your project and why you wish to speak with them in particular. You may need to reassure them that they have something valuable to add. Some people may like to have a family member or a friend present, and you should go along with such a request. Depending on the conversational etiquette and expectations of the people concerned, two interviewees, talking together with occasional prodding from the investigator, can produce wonderful material. An interview with a single individual can also create a strong dynamic and lead to rich material being recorded.

You should be very courteous to any potential interviewee, aware that they are doing you a generous favour. Take with you a small offering such as a cake, a packet of biscuits – or a document from your research that they might find of interest. Choose a place to meet where they feel comfortable. An interview conducted in their home can be very worthwhile because there will often be memory triggers nearby, things like photographs, letters, maybe a painting. Ask whether such things are available. Prompts like these can be a great way of starting an interview in a more relaxed way.

Take a consent form with you. Its content may be dictated by your institution, but it should have a section explaining the nature of the project terms, and then a series of statements setting out the conditions under which you may make use of the material in the interview. You should show the interviewee the consent form either beforehand or right at the beginning of the interview, and ask them to sign it then or straight after the interview is over.

Chat with your interviewee in a friendly way, but also explain you do not want to get into too much detail about the events to be discussed until the interview proper starts. Otherwise, the best parts come out unrecorded. If the interview is in a private home, let the interviewee choose the room, but take time with the setting up. Ask where the power point is, but try not to boss them around – it's their house. A table can be helpful for setting up your recording device. Although it's not essential, an external microphone can greatly enhance sound quality. When you both feel ready to start, do a sound check. Ask your interviewee to state their name, the date and the place where the interview is being recorded, or do it yourself. Make sure you have some basic biographical details – birth year, locations lived, dates of marriage/s, children's birth dates, and so on, as details like this can help you with dates they may not include in their interview. It's often helpful to fill out some details in a notebook beforehand, or to begin the recording by asking some basic biographical questions.

While it's wise to have a list of topics and questions prepared, you need to be adaptable. Your interviewee or participant in the history-telling process may well want to tell his or her story in a particular way, developing the sequence of events, the plot line, with self-selected highlights. Sometimes this means going off on what seems to be a tangent, but you could learn something unexpected. Be patient. You can always throw in your question later.

Be an attentive listener. Listening can be tiring, but don't show it. Nod a lot, take notes, but remember the don'ts of interviewing.

Interviewing don'ts

- Don't talk too much; it will ruin your interview. Even 'listening responses' –'yes', 'mmm', 'oh', 'really?' – can be a little tedious to someone listening later. Silent nods are recommended.
- Never allow yourself to look bored or restless. Act enthusiastic; use facial expressions and body language positively.
- Do not butt in. Let interviewees finish what they have to say. Even if you need a particular detail, wait until they have finished their sentence.
- Do not ask leading questions. Keep your questions open-ended. For example, rather than 'Did you detest fighting in the war?' ask, 'Could you tell me about your war experience?' Instead of 'Did you like sailing to the Antarctic?' ask, 'What are some of your favourite recollections about sailing to the Antarctic?'
- Do not correct or contradict your interviewee. Do not take issue with them or suggest they are incorrect, even if you are sure of it.
- Do not expect interviewees to remember exact dates. If they get flustered trying to remember a date, you might help them out by suggesting that the decade would do, or that you could check this later, or that they could get back to you later on this.

Sometimes an oral history can become a grab-bag of disconnected stories. You need to ask *when* and *where* things happened and *who* exactly your interview is referring to. If they can't recall a date, asking how old they were at the time, or the relation between that event and a life cycle event (such as birth of a child, a marriage, a war) can help with periodisation.

It is recommended practice to send the transcript of interview to the interviewee for corrections. The process of *transcription* is time-consuming and can take you four times as long as the actual recording. Some historians pay experts to do this part of the work, but you need a budget allowance to do so. If the interview turns out not to be relevant, or not central to your research data, you could index it for key topics and themes, and selectively transcribe it. Interviewees usually appreciate receiving the transcript, and they often appreciate a copy of the tape too, which they can keep or give to a family member.

If your interviewee has lent you photographs or other documents, you have a very special obligation to return them very quickly and in good order. Taking a good digital camera along to the interview is useful, for it allows you to obtain copies immediately. Some people take a scanner. If your interviewee is agreeable, take a photograph of him or her, which you might wish to include in your written work. Be clear and informative about what you'll be doing with the copied and photographed material.

Sometimes a follow-up interview is desirable. Leave this possibility open, because when you play back the interview afterwards you may think of additional questions that need answering. Sometimes you can do this via mail or email. Occasionally an interviewee will realise they have more to reveal and will themselves request a follow-up.

Above all, respect your interviewee. Sometimes a good relationship can take a while to develop. Maybe the session will turn out to be a conversation about the past, not an interview as such. They are telling you their version of history, what they have experienced, so let them do it. Some topics will be emotional or awkward, and you may need to ask confronting questions. While these should not come too early in the piece, avoid judging too quickly that you should *not* ask such questions. Sometimes people are very willing to tackle the uncomfortable questions too. Use your discretion. This is a person-to-person relationship, and you need to use all your people skills.

Indigenous oral history is a particularly special kind of oral history, as are the histories of all those peoples who have no long tradition of literacy. Histories of this kind may be conveying encultured 'ancestral memories' going back multiple generations. You will be dealing with 'stories' that may seem mythologised, that are being told in a way unfamiliar to many westerners. It may not be first-hand history, but it will often contain a great deal of information plus conceptualisations and interpretations that can valuably inform your project. Indigenous history may also be analysed as a form of history-telling that can be critiqued and discussed. History-telling may be through song, dance, storytelling traditions, art, and many forms of popular culture transmitted between generations. Historians are only beginning to learn about and analyse these significant historiographical traditions.

If you are working with people who have suffered long histories of oppression, you as historian will need to take this into account because their initial response to you may be a test of your attitudes and character. If you are an 'insider' in such a group you may be more readily accepted, but there will still be issues and limitations.[16]

Building research relationships with other people can be time consuming, but it is well worth it. A good historian must obtain insider perspectives to truly understand the past. Most oral history deals with living memory and people's experiences during their lifetimes. Sometimes, however, you will be dealing with deeper stories – of landscape and human creation, perhaps of slave journeys, passed down the generations.

Once your project is complete, you should deposit your interview transcripts and tapes in a library or other collecting institution. You will have created a valuable piece of historical data which future researchers will have the benefit of using if it is stored safely.[17]

Ann Curthoys

I was living in Canberra at the time of the 2003 bushfires, when over 500 suburban homes were burnt down. In the end, my home turned out to be safe, but over several days the repeated warnings that the fires could change direction and return made me realise that the valuable materials in my study – including oral history tapes, as well as photographs, pamphlets, minutes of meetings, and other records from the Freedom Ride of 1965 that I'd written about in a book which appeared in 2002 – could well be destroyed. I asked the specialist library of the Australian Institute of Aboriginal and Torres Strait Islander Studies whether I could donate my material. They agreed, and so they are now available for anyone to use, and they are much safer than they could ever be with me.

When to stop researching

Some historians enjoy the detective aspect of research so much that they start their writing too late. While a 'long-awaited' book may be celebrated, expectant readers will not wait forever. Not only that, but someone else may beat you to the finish line, and your publisher will no longer want your work. Set a deadline for starting your writing, and another for finishing it. A submission deadline, an expression of interest from a journal editor or a publisher – any hard deadline set by someone else works wonders.

At some point, you have to write, and write, and write. There will always be another article, another book, if the subject is worth it. For now, let's write.

5

How to avoid writer's block

To think of all the years when I had nothing but time and yet wrote not one word. And now like some misplaced, misgendered Scheherazade, I am trying to stave the night off with a flying, fleeting pen …
AMITAV GHOSH, *THE HUNGRY TIDE*[1]

In that space where research and writing overlap, a marvellous creative process starts to kick in. You have absorbed so much information; some of it seems relevant, even crucial, some less so. Yet you read all that material and took those notes because you found it fascinating. Perhaps you hoped you would see an obvious thread linking all those disparate pieces of information. But the neural pathways in your brain *are* starting to make connections. Whether this happens subconsciously, in your sleep, during bouts of insomnia or while cleaning the kitchen is irrelevant. Your historical mind is busy at work. Sometimes you will find yourself staring at a blank computer screen or an unblemished sheet of paper. A morning of inertia – where you are seemingly 'doing nothing' – can quite often lead to

1. Fixing a writing problem

I DON'T LIKE MY CHAPTER/ESSAY, ETC. ANY MORE

It sounds like you've lost your direction. You don't know what you want to say or how to say it.

SUGGESTION: Think back to when and why you started. What excited you? What did you hope to achieve when you started the project? Perhaps show your writing to a trusted friend, for honest feedback. Maybe there *is* something wrong, or maybe you've just lost confidence in a piece of writing that is actually quite good.

a creative explosion in the afternoon. Consequently, many writers suspect that 'doing nothing' may actually allow the brain to sort the ideas into files and creatively connect ideas.

Most of us have found it hard to write at some time or another. We have done a lot of research, we have some ideas – but the words won't come. We delay and procrastinate, and find dozens of things to do – except sitting down and writing. We just have to make that trip to the garden centre, fix those things around the house that suddenly can't be left any longer, answer emails that really aren't important, students need our urgent attention, a film just must be seen – anything not to write. Or perhaps we *do* sit down; we write an opening paragraph, only to delete it. We write another one, and delete that too. Somehow we can't get started, just can't work out what it is we want to say.

So, how do we get past writer's block, these patterns of avoidance, of procrastination, of dissatisfaction? We are assuming here that you have done all the background work – some substantial primary research, the organisation of your materials, and the planning of your chapters (discussed in chapter 7). If you haven't done all this, it's no wonder you can't get started, and it's probably silly to try. If you have, and still the words won't come, there are various strategies you can use to break the impasse. Here are a few suggestions.

Where to write

First, make sure you have an appropriate setting in which to write. For most people it will be a table or desk at which you feel comfortable, and where no one will interrupt you during your scheduled 'writing time'. In his useful book *The Common Writer*, Robert Neale tells us of the methods some writers use to get their ideas flowing and put themselves into a proper writing mood. Rudyard Kipling, apparently, demanded extremely black ink and a particular kind of pen, and could not express himself using a pencil.[2] Jack Kerouac famously insisted on using a particular brand of typewriter.[3] These days, most people find a computer is essential. You may have a private office, or a quiet study at home; you might prefer to take your laptop to your local coffee shop, or to a hidden corner desk in the library. The point is that you need a writing space where you can avoid interruption.

And inevitably, if there are children in the equation, they will want your attention the minute you sit down to write.

Ann McGrath

School holiday scenario. Everyone gets up late. 8 am: I take dog for walk, shower, eat breakfast, clean up, get dressed, finally I start writing; it's 9.30. At 10.30 teenager gets up. Wheedles: 'Mum, can you *please* cook me bacon and eggs?' Impressed that she isn't wanting McDonald's, I cook. Serve. Clean up. Then: 'Can you please make me a carrot juice?' Extremely healthy choice. Make juice – 4 mins. Wash up juicer parts – 12 mins. 'Can *you* clean up the rest?' I ask, aware that this could create a conflict situation and risk emotional energy being wasted that could suck out writing energy.

Teenager: 'No, I have to get ready now. Oh, and I can't go out unless you get the internet fixed – I have to print out a VIP ticket so I can get into the movie.'

Stressed writer gets assertive: 'Can't *you* ring the internet people?'

'No way! I've hardly got time to straighten my hair and do my makeup.'

'Look, *I* can't phone about the internet. I haven't got two hours to spare being switched between Sydney, Tasmania, Mumbai and Kolkata just so you can print out a movie ticket.'

Pathetic wails, angst, agony. Then: 'What about my schoolwork if the internet is down? I'm going back to school soon! I'll fail all my subjects.'

The ultimate blackmail line – it works like a dream. I'm calling the phone company.

When I'm home, to my daughter I *look* like I'm on holidays. And she knows, as all children know, that she is my number one job. If I'm in sight, I'm in danger – or at least my writing is.

In earlier generations, and perhaps still, some men have had secluded offices where nobody could disturb them. Manning Clark had a legendary upstairs study reached only by an inhumanly narrow, steep ladder. This created a definite division between house and office. He also had a wife to keep his several children away. However, those of us doing double duty as writers and carers are unlikely to construct ladders to our offices – it would be too difficult to check on the rice, the roast and the children who might be climbing into cupboards and doing taste tests on rat poison.

When to write

Make sure that you really do have *writing time* and that you keep it for writing and only writing. You will need more time than you imagine. Getting it right is usually a slow process, and there is always some wasted time. If you know you have to go to a meeting in half an hour, it's unlikely you'll get into the rhythm, and even if you do you won't have time to see your train of thought through.

Let's face it, you want to write. You will judge yourself on your success, and so will others. You will get frustrated with lack of progress. So don't let everything else intrude. Sometimes things are too important, and yes, of course go to the doctor, talk soothingly to the colleague threatening to jump off the roof, feed your children. Many things can wait, though, including the dishes, the laundry and washing the dog. Your writing just has to come first at times – or you will never do it.

It's important to plan writing time. How much and when depends on your circumstances – whether you are a full-time writer, a part-time writer, an academic with lots of teaching and administrative demands, and/or have children or elderly parents to care for. How and where you find writing time is an individual matter. Some people advise writing every day, but neither of us has ever had the kind of life that made that possible. A variant of this advice is to set yourself a daily target, say 1000 words, and stop when you reach it. This seems to work for a number of people, so by all means try it, but it's never worked for either of us. What does work, we find, is to schedule a particular block of time for writing on certain days, and to stick to the schedule as closely as we can.

Find the time of day when you write best. Ann McGrath finds the morning best, between 9 and 12.30. She has an energy lull around 3 pm. A little catnap often helps. (A student once caught one of our colleagues fast asleep on the office floor around this time of day.) Ann locks her door, but some people just keep on knocking anyway. While she finds it hard to write at night, it's easy to read something relevant that will help get the writing going the next day. Tired evenings are good times to read the article you didn't allow to interrupt the flow during the day. Or to read an inspiring book like *How to Write History that People Want to Read*. Seriously though, *reading* about writing is a total refresher when you're tired of actually doing it.

Ann Curthoys writes best between about 10 am and 7 pm, on her writing days. With a grown-up son, and a husband who also writes, the house is peaceful and set up for the task. She sometimes writes at night when the deadline is fierce, or when she gets so involved in a particular piece she can't stop. But usually she writes during the day.

A friend of ours used to get up very early. Without getting changed, she'd arm herself with some nuts, go up to her attic study, and work for a set length of time, for at least two hours, before she did anything else. She had to do her writing first, definitely before breakfast, before showering, before everything. Another colleague got her book done, along with holding down a demanding job and

2. Fixing a writing problem

I'VE REWORKED IT AND I'VE TWEAKED IT, BUT NOW I'M STUCK AND I DON'T KNOW WHAT TO DO

SUGGESTION 1: Time to talk to someone about what you are doing. Talking aloud often jolts you into working through the problem and seeing a way out. Hearing someone else 'get it' and articulate your idea is also exciting. Even hearing yourself explain it can provide a revelation.

SUGGESTION 2: Set it aside for a day or two, and then come back to it. Refreshed, your writing solutions will come to you.

3. Fixing a writing problem

IT JUST SEEMS LIKE A WHOLE LOT OF FACTS OR DISCONNECTED STORIES

The big ideas you started with have become obscured by so much detail that you can't see the big picture any more. You need to find a theme or thread that draws your material together. You need to find your own big story.

SUGGESTIONS: If it's a book chapter, think of how it fits into the book, what job it is doing in relation to the other chapters. If it's a journal article, view it as a draft and work out what your key argument is. Then restructure it accordingly, building in a strong argument as you rewrite it.

caring for two children, by always getting up before daybreak and working solidly for three hours.

Finding focus

You need to keep your focus firmly on your project, this task, this piece of writing you are about to do. People have different ways of finding focus. We have found that the best way to write is to have to work to a deadline – a paper for a seminar or conference, a book, a chapter. It pushes you along when otherwise you might rather let it slide. 'I'm working to a tight deadline' is not only a good excuse to get out of tasks that will stop you writing, but is also a good way to work. There is nothing like a looming finish time to get you going – and fast.

Walking is a common way to settle your thoughts. Mark Tredinnick starts off his *Little Red Writing Book* with a walk.[4] Charles

Darwin strolled along his English garden walk, each day marshalling his ideas before writing. According to the essayist Hazlitt, the poet Wordsworth 'always wrote (if he could) walking up and down a straight gravel-walk' and his friend Coleridge 'liked to compose in walking over uneven ground, or breaking through the straggling branches of a copse-wood'.[5] A bush walk, a walk anywhere, will get you in a different kind of rhythm.

We both like walking along the beach – it takes you away from everyday details and into another space, something larger, sometimes tranquil, sometimes restless, where you connect with the wider elemental flows. Waves and sand and rocks can make you meditative. (This only works, though, if you have a writing space nearby.) Perhaps nature stimulates our bodies and minds with its twists and turns, its rhythms, as the skies and the tides change. We see things afresh. And that's a good thing, as our eyes have grown accustomed to focusing no further than arm's length – on a screen or a text. To look out at distant vistas and horizons refreshes tired eyes and minds and heightens mental acuity. Wild, scouring winds and open spaces can blow away fears and narrow thoughts. If you take the time to observe, your garden or your local park can also be full of surprises. Nature's poetry seems to reawaken our own poetics.

When you are having trouble writing, ask yourself what is holding you back. Is it fear? Fear of what? Of issues you refuse to address? Decisions you've been unable to make? Of what someone will think? Who, if anyone, will publish your work? Confront your fears. Talking them out can be amazing therapy. Sometimes you can't discuss these issues in person, but perhaps you can share them with your readers. That's another kind of conversation.

Or perhaps you haven't sufficiently worked out your ideas. Maybe the problem is not the writing, but insufficient preparation. You may need to read more, learn more, and then try writing again.

Getting down to it

You have decided roughly what you want to say, done your research, read over your notes, and got yourself in the mood in an appropriate place with a healthy block of time at your disposal. By now you should know how long your final essay, chapter or book is going to be, how much time you have to write it, and thus be able to calculate how much you'll need to do each writing day if you are to meet your deadline. Set yourself a modest target for your first session, say 500 words, or perhaps five really good sentences.

If you are writing a book, you'll need to make chapter plans (we talk about this in more detail in chapter 7). However good your plan, you will probably change it as you go along. Some chapters become two, others may coalesce. Nevertheless, the plan is an important guide; it helps set goals, helps you know how much there is still to do.

Ann McGrath

I'm not good on chapter plans. My chapters grow, mutate and convolute, and I have to try to work out where they are leading. I would rather be more organised, but this is the way it is. It's a habit that has disconcerting moments, but seems to work out in the end. Maybe the element of surprise, or of not being too prescriptive about the road I am going to travel, adds to the excitement of writing history creatively – or so I hope.

Now sit yourself down, and *just write*. There are many different approaches to actually writing. Different methods suit different people. All that matters is that they work.

One way to get started is to type out all the preliminary bits first. For a book you need a title page, acknowledgments, contents page and a preface. For a conference paper it's the title, the name, place, and date of the conference, and your name. And so on, depending what it is. By the time you've done this, you are writing, you are on your way.

Another way of getting started is to write whatever comes into your head that's relevant to your topic. Then build up a paragraph or two, so you have something to work with, something to improve. Suddenly you can see how it should start, and you're away. A colleague of ours, on the other hand, never writes that way. He does all the research, then starts planning the writing in his head, occasionally jotting down thoughts in the middle of a conversation, brooding around the house, drifting in and out of conversations, very preoccupied. After a few days of this, he sits down and writes polished prose from the beginning – and keeps going to the end. No drafts. He pretty much keeps to his plan. It may not really be any easier than working things out with written chapter plans, but it works for him.

History-writing personality types

Perhaps you will recognise yourself in one of these history-writing personality types:

- *Mental historian*. You like to have all your ideas worked out before you start to write.
- *Write-thinking historian*. You only work out what you really want to say when you start writing.
- *Oral-thinker*. You cannot work out what you want to write about until you hear yourself talk it out with someone willing to listen.

- *Write-early historian*. You like to start writing at the same time as you are finding your first primary materials.
- *Data dumper*. You like to 'dump' all your primary sources in a big draft, which is like a fact sheet or story sheet of your findings. Then you go over it and make a new draft. And only then do you work out structure and argument.
- *Staged writer*. You do the research, then go methodically from one section to the next as you write.
- *Over-diligent researcher*. You won't start writing until you have found every source possible and researched exhaustively.
- *Literature historian*. You start formulating your work when you are reading other historians' work in related fields. Now you know how you differ from what's already in print.
- *Padding historian*. You write out your story in skeleton form, then pad it out with detailed information, examples and quotes.
- *Draw-up and colour-in historian*. You jot down some themes, ideas and possible arguments. You map out key facts and directions. Then you start to fill things in and gain more of an idea of what you want to say.
- *Story/meaning historian*. You write a narrative story style and then integrate some analysis.
- *Theory padder*. You work out the theory then add the data.
- *Data transformer*. You work out the data then come up with the theory.
- *Poetic paragrapher*. You think of a rich visual metaphor for what you want to say and work up a poetic first paragraph.

There are many more historical personality types out there, some still being invented. The main thing is that once you have got going, don't stop. Sure, take a day off, cope with the other parts of your life. But don't stop for too long. Keep going; give your writing a chance.

4. Fixing a writing problem

I'M AFRAID I'M NOT ON TOP OF THE RELEVANT SOURCES, THAT I HAVEN'T DONE ENOUGH RESEARCH

SUGGESTION 1: If this is true, go back to your research, start reading again. Reading can really get your thought processes going and contextualise your thinking.

SUGGESTION 2: Maybe you are just avoiding getting down to it. Rather than worrying about what you don't have, start sketching out what you *do* have. Then decide if you really need to do more research.

Finding friendly feedback

Often what we really need is encouragement. Someone else to say it's interesting. To care. To say something good about our writing. Everyone needs feedback and advice. Everyone.

There are various ways to get the feedback you need.

The student working on a thesis has a special right to seek advice, and has a supervisor from whom to seek that advice. If that's you, do listen and take advice. However, remember it is your thesis, not your supervisor's, and if there is some disputed aspect that you really want to keep, explain why it is important to your thinking. Perhaps you will come to some agreement. If you can't, think hard about why your supervisor disagrees with you. He or she might be right after all. It's a difficult balance, taking advice but at the same time staying in charge of your own project.

What about other kinds of feedback? Perhaps your institution runs writing workshops or special graduate student conferences. Sometimes graduate students form their own writing workshop groups. When we have run writing workshops for doctoral students, we set up opportunities for writing groups. Each student had to prepare a draft chapter of their thesis and circulate it to everyone else. Students were encouraged to engage with the author over what they really thought. At the same time, we insisted that they be respectful, and asked them to ensure that criticism be constructive. Their first comment was to be about an aspect of the writing 'that really worked'. After the workshops, students set up their own email networks, where they swapped references, tips and ideas and kept up with each other's progress. We know of two students who fell in love; others made lifelong friends; several later gained good positions on the strength of their theses.

You only need two people to start a group. Two doctoral students we know meet every Monday morning at one's kitchen table to sit down and write. This is the 'writing companion model'. For the first two or three hours, they do not speak; they write. Then they swap what they've written and critique each other's work. This strategy could be especially important if you are procrastinating – for here you do have someone looking over your shoulder, as well as an in-

5. Fixing a writing problem

IT'S JUST NOT FLOWING!

Sometimes flow problems simply mean that you haven't worked something out yet. You haven't quite decided what is relevant, what is central to your purpose and what is not.

SUGGESTION 1: Go back to your primary sources. Or secondary sources. Just make sure this isn't time-wasting or procrastination.

SUGGESTION 2: Talk to others to help you with conceptual stumbling blocks. They are not there to solve your writing problem for you, but simply speaking aloud to someone about your work can help you see what you need to do next.

house critic who can offer encouragement and advice. The reciprocal element means that most people will behave well in this situation. They enter the arrangement voluntarily, believing the other has something to offer. They have much to gain from it.

It isn't only PhD students who need feedback. Most of us need it, at least some of the time. Peer critique is valuable. Your peers know what they like to read. They bring fresh eyes to your work and can tell you what they find appealing and what they don't. They can help draw you out and help you jump over conceptual or stylistic obstacles. You can also have a good old grumble to someone going through the same thing, but always with the main goal of improving your drafts and getting on to the next writing task.

You can participate in a support group with people undertaking a writing project similar to yours – use email, chat networks, Facebook and other interactive platforms. If you live in the same town, a scheduled coffee or lunch meeting where you focus on your work, reading each other's drafts beforehand, can be very helpful. It also creates a deadline for you to meet.

Attending seminars and presenting conference papers are standard ways of getting feedback on ideas and argument, less often on the quality of the writing. Delivering a paper helps you see problems not only in argument or research, but also in writing style and structure.

6. Fixing a writing problem

MY WRITING IS FLOWING BUT I REALISE I NEED TO DO MORE RESEARCH

SUGGESTION: **No, don't stop; let the river run until it reaches a dam. Only then can you do that extra research. If the writing is flowing, don't stop for anything except floods, other life-threatening emergencies and occasional sustenance.**

Reading your work aloud can give you a whole new sense of it. When it comes to the question and discussion time, ask a friend or colleague to jot down the questions you are asked – you'll be too busy with the answers. Some people get very nervous about the questions they might get, and how to answer them. It's always better to get questions, even if they are difficult to answer on the spot. Here are some strategies for dealing with the difficult ones:

- 'Well, that is very helpful; I hadn't thought of it that way at all. That really provides food for thought.'
- 'So where could I find out more about that?'
- 'I'd like to discuss this further after the session.'
- Use your answer to say more of what you'd like to say, but don't ignore the question entirely.

Seminars and conferences have other benefits. You can find relevant new contacts, new ideas, new readings, and various people offering helpful advice. Someone may even offer to publish your work, or suggest you put it into a competition, a collection of readings, whatever. Sometimes industry elders will tell you it is terrific. We know of some historians who rarely or never gave seminar or conference papers; in nearly every case, their research gradually suffered, as they lost their sense of audience and of a scholarly community. It is remarkable how much the written and spoken word are intertwined, even now, and how much face-to-face contact can influence our thinking, our connections, and our writing.

Above all, when you've got that feedback and taken it into account (or not), get back to your work and get it finished. Send it to your publisher or journal. Get your history out to the people of today. It may sound strange, but if you leave it, history can date very quickly.

7. Fixing a writing problem

I'M BORED WITH MY TOPIC

SUGGESTION: Finish what you are doing as soon as possible. Leave it for a while; perhaps you've been working too hard. When you feel refreshed, read it over. If you still don't find it interesting, it may need reconceptualising.

Collaborative writing

One surefire way of getting and giving feedback is to write with one or two other authors. Collaborative writing can have other advantages, too. You can produce something you could not do on your own through bringing together different kinds of expertise. This works especially well in interdisciplinary work, say, working with a literary critic, a lawyer or a political scientist, but it can also work well when both writers are historians. You do lose individual control to a certain extent, but you gain a lot in mixing your expertise, and in general support and encouragement.

Every collaboration is different, because the personalities and skills and approaches of the co-authors vary. The common factor, in our experience, is that you finish the project because you don't want to disappoint your co-author. Having someone else at the other end of the email waiting for your chapter means you simply *have* to write. It's the best medicine for writer's block that we know.

6

Once upon a time

BEGINNINGS AND ENDINGS

The King of Hearts' advice to Alice:
'Begin at the beginning ⋯ and go on till
you come to the end: then stop.'
LEWIS CARROLL, *ALICE'S ADVENTURES IN WONDERLAND*[1]

It's Saturday. You go to the best bookshop in town. Look around at the books – the exciting new hardbacks and the stylish, bestselling paperbacks. They look so enticing and appealing. Matt and shiny covers feature dramatic titles hustling to grab your attention. Sometimes the titles make promises beyond what the books deliver, so you may be a little wary. You pick up one that interests you, and check out the beginning. Can you judge whether it will be a good read, and what topics and eras this book spans?

Beginnings matter to readers of all kinds. If the opening is not enticing, the reader may not continue. Editors, too, often decide very quickly on whether a manuscript works. Any thesis examiner or editor will tell you that the beginning matters more than any other part of a manuscript. They will read the whole thesis, but usually they know very quickly if they are going to pass or fail it – the opening pages tell them how well the writer is in charge of what he or she is writing, is in command of the subject, the material, the argument. In short, opening sentences, paragraphs and chapters matter.

There are many different ways to begin. Some people start by outlining issues or problems, others with an anecdote that leads into the history to be narrated and analysed, and yet others by setting the scene geographically. There is no 'right' or proper way to begin. You can look at the options, explore their strengths and limitations, and choose opening gambits to suit your purpose. Your beginning doesn't always have to be where or quite how you might think one should 'normally' begin. Be creative.

So, let's begin at the beginning, and that is with the title.

Book titles

Books live and die by their titles, especially books by lesser known authors. They really, really matter. Sometimes they are very hard to dream up; at other times, they come to you before you even start writing the book. Sometimes publishers are very helpful, suggesting better titles than you could have thought of yourself.

There is no formula for finding a good title. Here we consider the different types of titles we've found for history books. One of these types might be just right for yours.

Popular titles

Look up any large library catalogue and you will find hundreds of titles that start with *A Short History of …*

Then there are the books that start with a year:

1815: The Roads to Waterloo by Gregor Dallas (2001)

1968: The Year That Rocked the World by Mark Kurlansky (2005)

'Decline and fall' titles are especially popular. Most famously:

Decline & Fall of the Roman Empire by Edward Gibbon (six volumes, 1776–89)

Alluded to in:

The Decline and Fall of the British Empire, 1781–1997 by Piers Brendon (2008)

Just as popular is the closely related genre of 'rise and fall' titles:

The Rise and Fall of the Third Reich: A History of Nazi Germany by William L. Shirer (1960)

The Rise and Fall of Anne Boleyn: Family Politics at the Court of Henry VIII by Retha M. Warnicke (1991)

Sometimes it's reversed, to good effect:

A Peculiar Imbalance: The Fall and Rise of Racial Equality in Early Minnesota by William D. Green (2007)

Or used somewhat wryly:

The Rise and Fall of Marvellous Melbourne by Graeme Davison (1978)

Then we have the 'hidden history' titles:

The Hidden History of the Korean War, 1950–1951: A Nonconformist History of Our Times by I.F. Stone (1988)

The Hidden History of the Secret Ballot by Romain Bertrand, Jean-Louis Briquet and Peter Pels (2007)

There are just as many 'untold story' titles:

The Brother: The Untold Story of the Rosenberg Case by Sam Roberts (2003)

The Road to Rescue: The Untold Story of Schindler's List by Mietek Pemper and David Dollenmayer (2008)

There are the 'triumph' titles:

The Colour Bar: The Triumph of Seretse Kama and His Nation by Susan Williams (2008)

And the 'myth' titles:

The Myth of 1648: Class, Geopolitics and the Making of Modern International Relations by Benno Teschke (2003)

The Myth of the Great Depression by David Potts (2008)

One form that academics like is the two-pronged title, with a snappy or arresting phrase followed by a long descriptive subtitle that tells us what the book is about. The first half of such a title might be mood-building:

Somme Mud: The Experiences of an Infantryman in France, 1916–1919 by E.P.F. Lynch (2008)

Ochre and Rust: Artefacts and Encounters on Australian Frontiers by Philip Jones (2007)

Or attention-grabbing:

The Architect of Genocide: Himmler and the Final Solution by Richard Breitman (1992)

Ordered to Die: A History of the Ottoman Army in the First World War by Edward J. Erickson (2000)

One of the most famous examples of this style of title is:

The Cheese and the Worms: The Cosmos of a Sixteenth Century Miller by Carlo Ginzburg (1976)

A variant of this approach is to start with a quotation, or a pretend quotation, followed by a descriptive subtitle. Examples include:

Tell the Court I Love My Wife: Race, Marriage and Law – An American History by Peter Wallenstein (2002)

Through a Howling Wilderness: Benedict Arnold's March to Quebec, 1775 by Thomas A. Desjardin (2007)

Ann McGrath

I called my first book *Born in the Cattle: Aborigines in Cattle Country*. I was going to call it 'Growing Up on the Stations' but someone else wrote a political study with a similar title. An old man named Essy, whom I met in a remote town called Kununurra, in northern Australia, had introduced himself thus: 'I was born in the cattle, amongst the horses, just like Jesus.' This statement indicated an identity associated with a colonising era, where cattle culture and introduced religion had transformed his traditional country. So there was my title.

Popular history books can have two-pronged titles too, often with a long subtitle making some kind of very large claim. Dava Sobel seems to have set off something of a fashion with her hugely popular *Longitude: The True Story of a Lone Genius who Solved the Greatest Scientific Problem of his Time* (1996). This style of title has been followed by many others, such as Simon Winchester, with *The Professor and the Madman: A Tale of Murder, Insanity, and the Making of the Oxford English Dictionary* (1999) and, more recently, Iain McCalman in *Darwin's Armada: How Four Voyagers to Australasia Won the Battle for Evolution and Changed the World* (2009).

Of course, this is just one kind of title, and if all titles were like this it would get very tiresome. There are many other kinds. Some books have simpler titles:

England in the Eighteenth Century by J.H. Plumb (1963)

Straightforward titles, too, can be quite enticing:

Murder of a Medici Princess by Caroline Murphy (2008)

Titles asking a question usually work well, though these are not so common. See:

What is History? by Edward Hallet Carr (1967)

Why Weren't We Told? by Henry Reynolds (1999)

Who was John F. Kennedy? by Yona Zeldis McDonough, Jill Weber and Nancy Harrison (2005)

Historians love alliterative titles, and sometimes these work well too. They can also sometimes sound a little obvious and predictable. What do you think of the following?

Lincoln's Land: The History of Abraham Lincoln's Coles County Farm by Kurt W. Peterson (2009)

Hope Against History: The Course of Conflict in Northern Ireland by Jack Holland (1999)

All of these methods can work. Beware, though, of titles that are hard to say or remember, titles that sound like clichés, titles that borrow from other titles and not in a good way, and titles that are just too smart by half. We have our doubts about:

Rasputin: The Saint Who Sinned

Killing Hitler: The Plots, the Assassins, and the Dictator Who Cheated Death

Journal article titles

Journal article titles are also important, not so much for catching attention in general as for catching the attention of those most likely to be interested in the contents. Some of the best-known historical essays have titles that intrigue and inform.

Let's look at the titles of the most cited articles in some respected history journals. While we are certainly not suggesting they are cited purely because of their titles, the titles do help attract attention. (The subject and the reputation of the author are usually more important selling points.) In February 2009 the most cited articles in the *Journal of British Studies* were titled:

- Rethinking the Public Sphere in Early Modern England
- Britishness and Otherness: An Argument
- One Big Thing: Britain, Its Empire and Their Imperial Culture

All very direct, informative and stimulating, we think. In the *European History Quarterly*, the top three cited articles that same month were:

- The Persecution of the Jews in the Netherlands: A Comparative Western European Perspective
- 'Imagined Communities' and the Origins of the National Question in the Balkans
- Jean-Baptiste Colvert and the Origins of the Dutch War

Not quite so intriguing, perhaps, but still informative, the *Journal of Modern History*'s top three cited articles in February 2009 were:

- Goodbye to Tristes Tropes: Ethnography in the Context of Modern World History
- 'Making Whole What has Been Smashed': Reflections on Reparations
- Phantasies of the Public Sphere: Rethinking the Habermas of Historians

These nine titles show the various means specialist historians use to attract attention to what they have written. The most common, perhaps, is the two-sided title with an interesting but very general first half ('Goodbye to Tristes Tropes', 'One Big Thing', and so on), and the explanatory second half that tells you what the essay is about. Also important, though, are words such as 'rethinking', 'argument', 'reflections', suggesting this essay will not simply contain new information but will offer some new ways of thinking about its subject, challenging received approaches.

Chapter titles

If vague titles don't help a book to sell, vague chapter titles don't help either. How many times have you picked up a book, not sure whether to buy it or not, scanned the chapter titles, and thought, 'Well I still don't know what this book is about', and put it down? Or, you do own the book, but the chapter titles provide no guidance whatsoever as to how the book is organised.

These chapter titles come from a book about colonial administrator Edward Gibbon Wakefield and his brothers. They are rather beautiful, but as to what they are about, the reader has no idea. The book is in four parts, and here is Part Two:

Part Two: Forward, Forward Let Us Range, 1828–1839

7. This Black Place

8. A Castle in the Air

9. Life as Propaganda

10. A Long and Sore Trial

11. Down the Ringing Grooves of Change

12. Strangers to their Family

13. The Ingenious Projector

14. 'I would die in your service'

15. Possess Yourselves the Story

Chapter titles can also use the double-headed approach discussed above in relation to book titles. Joy Damousi does this to good effect in her prize-winning book, *Freud in the Antipodes: A Cultural History of Psychoanalysis in Australia*. Her chapter titles include:

2: 'I can speak if the listener will be patient': Listening to the shell-shocked

8: 'Europe's loss is Australia's gain': The advent of institutes of psychoanalysis in Australia, 1940s and 1950s

Bruce Dorsey's *Reforming Men and Women: Gender in the Antebellum City* goes for economy and simplicity. In context, these chapter headings are informative:

1. Gender and Reformers in the New Republic
2. Poverty
3. Drink
4. Slavery
5. Immigration

The preface

Traditionally the preface is where the historian speaks in a personal voice, explaining perhaps how he or she came to this project. Frequently it is the best-written part of the whole thesis or book, for the author suddenly finds it easy to write freely and directly, in the active voice, without equivocation. An aspect of personal experience often draws us to particular topics, and the reader appreciates knowing what that something is. A scholarly interest in questions of race and ethnicity, for example, nearly always comes from something in a person's background, such as involvement in protest politics, witnessing racial discrimination or membership of a minority group. Personal experience, or awareness of the experiences of friends or family members, may prompt an interest in histories of grief, suffering or mourning. Those with political sympathies with labour movements and parties will often write labour and working class history. Keep this personal account fairly brief, though; if it's not to the point, it can sound merely self-indulgent.

An excellent example of a personal start to a history book comes in Catherine Hall's *Civilising Subjects: Metropole and Colony in the English Imagination 1830–1867*. It begins:

> The origins of this book lie in my own history. I was born in Kettering, Northamptonshire, in 1946. My father, John Barrett, was a Baptist minister, my mother a budding historian who had become a clergyman's wife.

After explaining her own intellectual journey as a feminist historian increasingly interested in the question of race, she describes a visit with her Jamaican-born husband to Jamaica in 1988:

> Driving along the north coast of Jamaica that summer of 1988 … we came to the small village of Kettering. I was immediately struck by its name, and by the large Baptist chapel with the name of William Knibb, the Emancipator, blazoned upon it. … This was the beginning of an unravelling of a set of connected histories linking Jamaica with England, colonised with colonisers, enslaved men and women with Baptist missionaries, freed people with a wider public of abolitionists in the metropole.[2]

Already we are intrigued and want to read more.

Here's a preface we think much less inviting. It comes from a companion to European decolonisation. There is no introduction, so the only explanation of what the text hopes to achieve is in the two-paragraph preface. Here's the first paragraph:

> The book covers only the European maritime empires. Two other great empires were created in the eighteenth/nineteenth centuries.

The Russian empire expanded into Central Asia. Arguably this did not differ from the maritime expansion of Western Europe and it has dissolved in not dissimilar ways since 1989. The United States, itself the successor state of various European empires, acquired a huge land mass and some overseas possessions in the nineteenth century. This too can be seen as part of the same process of European expansion. Some parts of the American empire have also been decolonized, for example the Philippines in 1946.[3]

There are more enticing ways to indicate what you are *not* doing that at the same time quickly introduce the reader to what is distinctive about your project. John Hobson's preface to *The Eastern Origins of Western Civilisation* (2004) starts this way:

> To reassure my potential reader who thinks anxiously, 'not another typical book on the rise of the West', let me say this is not one such book. For unlike almost all the books on this topic, this one does not recount all the familiar themes according to the standard European, ethnocentric frame of reference. In place of the usual story, I produce one that brings the East into the limelight.[4]

The introduction

One effective style of introduction is to state your main idea strongly, and indicate that the rest of the book will show how you came to this idea, the details and complexities that have arisen, and the ins and outs of the story. That is, hold something back, create interest, but still tell the reader your main idea, your overall approach, the big picture. The interest will be in finding out how you got there, why you think this idea helps us understand something about the past that has not been understood before.[5]

Be positive. Too often, introductions dwell on what the writer has *not* done, and have a slightly defensive tone. Of course you have not done everything – just outline what you *have* done, and give reasons.

A good introduction may establish a problem, something the following history will need to explain. You can establish tension, drawing attention to two or more different ways of understanding the same event, movement or historical figure. You might begin by outlining what other historians have written on your topic, and how you are going to add something new. For example, in his study of the origins of the American involvement in Vietnam, historian Mark Lawrence begins by outlining the various arguments that have been put so far. These include the view that Americans saw Vietnam as part of a global pattern of communist aggression against the West; that America saw the region as of economic value; and that involvement in Vietnam was a product of domestic American politics. Lawrence says, 'All three arguments hold merit, and none excludes the others … Nonetheless, this scholarship falls short of offering a satisfactory explanation of American behaviour.' He follows this with a statement of his own approach: 'This book offers a fresh look at the origins of US involvement in Vietnam by treating the United States as just one participant in a complicated transnational deliberation over the destiny of Indochina.'[6]

You might begin by telling the reader about your research process. What material have you looked at? How did you find it? Has anyone else looked at it? Before the introduction to her book, *Two Worlds: First Meetings between Maori and Europeans, 1642–1772*, Anne Salmond has a three-page section called Research. She starts by telling the reader that her book really commenced with her travels to the *marae* (ceremonial centres) in various parts of the North Island of New Zealand, with two Maori elders, in the early 1970s. She continues:

As we travelled from one *marae* to another, we became immersed
in the rhythms of tribal time, the taste of food, the sound and lilt of
voices, the way people moved .... Great orators spoke, and the voices
of the *kai-karanga* (ceremonial callers) rang out across the marae.[7]

Already we are with her on her historical journey.

Very often, you will write the introduction last, when you
know what you have done. This is especially true if you are a 'write-
thinking' historian, who works out the argument in the process of
writing. Even if you do write your introduction first, be prepared to
revise it substantially when you have finished revising your chapters.
Only then can you be sure it does introduce what follows.

The first chapter

The first chapter usually takes the reader straight to the narrative.
Richard White begins the first chapter of his book, *The Middle
Ground: Indians, Empires, and Republics in the Great Lakes Region,
1650–1815*, with this:

> The Frenchmen who traveled into the *pays d'en haut*, as they called
> the lands beyond Huronia, thought they were discovering new
> worlds. They were, however, doing something more interesting.
> They were becoming co-creators of a world in the making.[8]

Iain McCalman has an intriguing and informative introduction in
*The Seven Ordeals of Count Cagliostro: The Greatest Enchanter of the
Eighteenth Century*.

> The greatest enchanter of the eighteenth century deserved better
> than this, I thought, looking at the house of Count Cagliostro,
> magician, alchemist, healer, and Freemason. It was a hole bashed

high in the side of a crumbling building, halfway along a tiny market lane in Palermo, Sicily. Behind the jagged brick outline you could dimly see the shell of a room, a dusty and derelict cave. The alley stank of urine.

It would be hard to find a sorrier memorial for someone who'd once been a household name throughout the western world, a magician whom monarchs had courted, bishops had feared, artists had painted, doctors had hated, and women had craved.[9]

These short first paragraphs give the reader a chance to 'be there', like McCalman was, fairly recently. You can see the decaying house of Cagliostro from the perspective of the author who is about to take you on a historical journey into his life. The author provides a sense not just of location and three-dimensional image, but also of smell. In a sentence, he tells you why this man is important, and about the passionate reactions to him. The pace is speedy and succinct. You anticipate that the author will not offer moral judgement, but instead will share a chance for you too to be seduced by a maestro enchanter.

This book could have been introduced quite differently, perhaps something like this:

This chapter opens my biographical study of an eighteenth century man who became well-known at the time as an alchemist. It starts with the family background that eventuated in his birth, and it then explores his achievements in the light of his associations with a range of contemporaries. His associates include women, medical experts, senior clergy and people in the arts. This study will pay special attention to royalty, class, gender, the state of medical science and other contemporary factors that gave rise to conflicts concerning chemistry/alchemy and that became especially pronounced between royalty, the church hierarchy, and other members of the ruling classes seeking to enhance their power and wealth.

Compared with McCalman's actual opening, this made-up paragraph makes no promises of fun, sensual pleasure or mystery. Based on this, readers would expect a certain solid, factual account, with evaluations, judgments and a neat line marking the end. They might learn something, but their imaginations will not be stretched.

Some histories begin with a description of place. We like Alan Atkinson's opening paragraphs in his book *Camden: Farm and Village Life in Early New South Wales*.

> Imagine Camden in January 1841, at the height of a dry summer. Take a good vantage point: if you are travelling from Sydney into the south country you can stop on the Cowpasture Bridge ... The bridge is wooden, a flat arch dating back to 1826, with dead leaves in its crevices. It was once highly thought of, well made and secure, but it has been much used since. Now, in summer 1841, it answers travellers like a lumpish low-voiced ostler, and it is a little weak in the centre where the boards have begun to rot.[10]

Others start by evoking the person at the centre of the history. Carlo Ginzburg's *The Cheese and the Worms* starts this way:

> His name was Domencio Scandella, but he was called Menocchio. He was born in 1532 (at his first trial he claimed he was fifty-two years old) in Montereale, a small hill town of the Friuli twenty-five kilometres north of Pordenone at the foot of the mountains. Here he had always lived, except for two years when he was banished following a brawl (1564–65).[11]

Already we know quite a bit about Menocchio, and want to know more.

Beginning with an anecdote

One of the most distinctive ways historians begin their books and essays is with an anecdote. Historians *love* the anecdote, that is, a short account of an entertaining or interesting incident, which in some way draws attention to the larger themes the historian will subsequently pursue. Repeatedly we have heard historians introduce seminar and conference papers with an anecdote. Countless essays and articles, chapters and books, begin with one. Other writers and scholars use them too, but none so insistently, frequently or purposefully as historians.

Anecdotes can be for fun, to engage attention, perhaps get a laugh. But for historians they have a more serious purpose: they suggest a desire to go beyond narrative to a larger analysis. If the historian's purpose were story-telling alone, the anecdote would probably be unnecessary; the longer story would itself suffice. It is because the historian, after telling the anecdote, wishes to go into more scholarly or analytical mode that the anecdote becomes important. It suggests a love of story, and holds out a promise of something reflective as well.

The anecdote has a long and distinguished history. In classical Greece and Rome it was thought to express something typical of a larger whole – as being true in general but not of any particular occasion.[12] Among the Romans, Plutarch in his *Lives* revealed character by illustrative anecdote and comment. In the 16th century, Michel de Montaigne's famous *Essays*, themselves influenced by Plutarch's *Lives*, only recently translated into French, elevated the use of anecdote to an art form. The essays have little structure. Sprinkled through them are anecdotes taken from ancient as well as contemporary authors and from popular lore.[13] In Russia, from the 17th century to the 20th, the anecdote rose to become a minor literary form of its own.

In more theoretically minded discourse, however, attitudes to the anecdote are not especially favourable. While appreciated for their brevity and piquancy, they are also questioned as having little or no historical or theoretical significance, as in the phrase 'mere anecdote'.

What all this means is that anecdotes only *seem* to be simple. They are in fact quite complex literary devices. Use them with care. If the anecdote is irrelevant, or not funny, it may well put readers off rather than entice them to read on. At their worst, anecdotes can send you off on the wrong track, making it hard for you to establish your conceptual framework or your argument, or to get your own voice back. At their best, they can excite your reader with a sense of 'truth'; they can stick in memory and leave an indelible impression.

Lyndal Roper uses anecdote very well. She begins her study of the witch craze in 17th century Germany with the story of an accusation of witchcraft. An old woman was standing in front of a cowshed during a harvest festival. The mistress of the house, afraid that the old woman would put a curse on her cows, 'screamed out "You shitty witch!" and the old woman fled home'. Roper goes on:

> It was done now: a public insult, the words uttered to her face,
> and heard by the audience of village revellers. There was no going
> back. Ursula Götz had been branded a witch, and only a trial could
> settle the issue. It was to take four years, but that trial sent the old
> woman to her death.[14]

A little later Roper writes: 'this book tells the story of those, like Ursula Götz, who died as witches; and the story of their accusers.'

Epigraphs

Filling some of the functions of the anecdote, the epigraph is the short quotation at the beginning of a book, chapter or essay which suggests something of what is to come. Epigraphs imply scholarship and learning. If there is more than one, they can be counterpointed, suggesting different and even contradictory aspects of the story or analysis to come. They can quickly give a feel for the times, themes, and people under examination. Mary Dudziak has one at the beginning of each chapter of her book, *Cold War, Civil Rights: Race and the Image of American Democracy*. Each epigraph is telling, such as the one for chapter 4, 'Holding the Line in Little Rock',[15] which reads:

> Little Rock has unfortunately become a symbol of Negro–White relations in the United States.
>
> AMERICAN CONSULATE, LOURENÇO MARQUESZ,
> MOZAMBIQUE TO DEPARTMENT OF STATE, SEPTEMBER 30, 1957.

Already we know that this chapter will tell us about US anxiety over the impact on its image abroad of this white racist demonstration. We are ready to read on.

Watch that signposting

It is important to let the reader know where you are going without boring them with excessive and repetitive signposting. We have read many PhD theses, and draft chapters, where the signposting is too frequent, heavy-handed and, in the end, irritating. It is important in introducing an essay or book to tell the reader what is the problem or issue you are going to explore, but you need to avoid repetition. Introductions should indeed give the reader an idea of what is to come, but not through a laborious listing of tasks. Don't say, 'This chapter will discuss the role of XX, and then the role of YY, and then develop an argument as to who was the more important'. You need to be more subtle. Perhaps say simply, 'Both XX and YY are important in this story, though in very different ways'.

Chapters that begin by reminding us what was in the last chapter are a no-no too – the reader has probably just read the last chapter, and has quite a good memory. Even if they have taken a break, most readers will remember what they have read, and if they do not, will probably quickly scan the last couple of pages before reading on.

Penelope Lively, a novelist whose characters often muse about history, begins her novel *Moon Tiger* at an old people's home. The narrator is Claudia Hampton, an elderly historian:

'I'm writing a history of the world,' she says. And the hands of the nurse are arrested for a moment; she looks down at this old woman, this old ill woman. 'Well, my goodness,' the nurse says. 'That's quite a thing to be doing, isn't it?'…

A history of the world. To round things off. I may as well – no more nit-picking stuff about Napoleon, Tito, the battle of Edgehill, Hernando Cortez … The works, this time. The whole triumphant murderous unstoppable chute – from the mud to the stars, universal and particular, your story and mine. I'm equipped, I consider; eclecticism has always been my hallmark. That's what they've said, though it has been given other names. Claudia Hampton's range is ambitious, some might say imprudent: my enemies. Miss Hampton's bold conceptual sweep: my friends.

… I shall omit the narrative. What I shall do is flesh it out; give it life and colour, add the screams and the rhetoric. Oh, I shan't spare them a thing. The question is, shall it or shall it not be linear history? I've always thought a kaleidoscopic view might be an interesting heresy. Shake the tube and see what comes out. Chronology irritates me. There is no chronology inside my head. I am composed of a myriad Claudias who spin and mix and part like sparks of sunlight on water.[16]

Historical framings are drawn from our own experiences of life and the world, so look at yourself and the world around you; challenge its limitations and preconceptions. A journal article will follow a house style and be more prescriptive. But, depending on the publication genre, your beginning doesn't always have to be where or quite how you think one should 'normally' begin. Be creative.

Endings

Endings are almost as important as beginnings. Essays, theses and journal articles should end strongly. After all the complexities and qualifications, all the pathways that we have travelled down, what can we say about our narrative and/or argument at the most general level? We have read too many PhD theses that end chapters, and then the whole thesis, by repeating things already said. This is just boring, and adds nothing. A conclusion needs to do something better than this. It should give the argument of the thesis or book at its most general and abstract level, at a level that has been implicit throughout but is now made quite explicit.

Emmanuel Le Roy Ladurie's *Carnival in Romans* (Romans is a town in southern France) ends by drawing out the larger meaning of the carnival in 1580 that his book has narrated:

> An isolated incident, the Carnival in Romans illuminates, reflects on the cultures and conflicts of an era. These include strictly urban struggles, municipal problems which set the craftsmen and the butcher trade in opposition to the patrician ruling group; traditional peasant agitation moulded into an assault on a system of land-holding that was becoming aggressive, capitalistic; the violent rejection of the government and taxes, both revealing of social conflict. There was also a place for the Catholic, medieval, Renaissance, and soon to be baroque folk traditions of festivity; the bourgeois, semi-learned and semi-egalitarian ideologies drawing inspiration from classical authors ...

He moves to an even higher level of generalisation in his last few sentences:

> The Carnival in Romans makes me think of the Grand Canyon. It shows, preserved in cross section, the social and intellectual strata and structures which made up a *très ancien régime*. In the twilight of the Renaissance it articulates a complete geology, with all its colours and contortions.[17]

Sometimes a conclusion can offer suggestions on where the work might lead next; that is, it opens out as much as it closes down. Where the story ends will dramatically change its meaning. If we are to take American historian Hayden White seriously, and recognise that the ending is chosen by the historian, not immanent in the events themselves, then different meanings of the events will be implied by ending the narrative at different points in time.[18] The history of the Second World War that ends in September 1945 will have a different meaning from one that takes the story up into the Cold War of the 1950s. A history that traces Holocaust memory right up to the 1990s and beyond, or which includes the story of what happened to former Nazis beyond the end of the war, will be different again. In his study of the French Revolution, Howard Brown makes this point very explicitly. 'Histories of the French Revolution,' he writes, 'that focus on democracy usually end in 1794, when the expansion of democratic ideology was halted and reversed, or in 1799, when the exercise of democratic practices was halted and reversed.' He goes on to argue for a later ending: 'That the Revolution did not end in 1794 or even 1799 is further confirmed by the persistence of endemic violence'.[19]

One possible and often appealing strategy is to go beyond the apparent ending or 'conclusion' and to trace how subsequent generations have remembered that story. That is, what is the afterlife of the original event? How has it affected us now, both within and outside our direct memory of it? In other words, extend the history towards the present and to present-day understandings of its relevance. The historian then has the opportunity to reflect on his or her journey and possibly to make a claim for its legacies in the present. In *Eye Contact: Photographing Indigenous Australians*, Jane Lydon tells of the 19th century European photographers who took extensive photographs of Indigenous people at a mission in Victoria.[20] Her final chapter shows how Indigenous people in this area have been recently using these photographs for a very different purpose, namely, to trace their genealogies, and to obtain information about traditional ways of life. The meaning of the photographs is still changing; the history is still unfolding in the present.

We like endings that somehow connect to the beginning, that help pull the whole thing together. Marcus Rediker does this in a moving way in his book, *The Slave Ship: A Human History*. In the introduction, he quotes the great African American scholar-activist W.E.B. DuBois, who called the slave ship voyages the 'most magnificent drama in the last thousand years of human history'. Rediker returns to this idea of a magnificent drama in his hopeful final paragraph. After referring to those enslaved people in Caribbean ports who cared for diseased and dying seamen, he concludes:

> These good deeds, taken by people who themselves had little enough food, shelter, health and space for ritual and burial, seemed to suggest the possibility of a different future. With their inspiration and our hard work, it may still be possible. The long, violent passage of the slave ship might finally come to an end, and the 'most magnificent drama' might become magnificent in an entirely new way.[21]

Les Carlyon, one of Australia's most popular historical writers, also does this in his book, *The Great War* (2006). He begins this way:

> There were so many of them, more than three hundred thousand, and we never really saw them. Not when it mattered to see them anyway, not when they were doing the things that marked them as different, then and now, from the rest of us.

He repeats these same ideas, and some phrases in the conclusion, 774 pages later.

> The Great War is long ago and far away ... All the Australians who fought on the western front are gone now. There were so many of them, and we never really saw them.[22]

Endings matter. More than anything else, it is the ending that the reader is most likely to remember. The ending offers a sense of completion, yet suggests further possibilities. It leaves the door open for a continuing history that will keep impacting and that will keep needing to be told.

7

Narrative, plot, action!

Historical narration without analysis is trivial,
historical analysis without narration is incomplete.
PETER GAY, *STYLE IN HISTORY*[1]

Most history books are in narrative form. They tell a story, and show
the movement of people and events through time. Usually, though,
that is not all they do – they also offer analysis and description.
Analysis helps us understand why things happened as they did; it
enables us to draw conclusions and comparisons, and to make some
generalisations. Description helps the reader imagine what places,
things and people in the past looked like, how people moved and
talked and acted, how they worked, did politics, played sport and
cared for each other. Those histories that at first glance *seem* to be in
another mode, to be non-narrative history, such as works of historical
argument and large-scale generalisation, usually still have a strong
component of narrative somewhere inside them.

The problem of how to combine narrative, analysis and
description confronts every history student, and every historian.

How chronological should I be, how thematic? How do I describe something that changes over time? Do I simply tell a story, or do I discuss what is happening, compare this story with other stories, draw conclusions? How do I make my story interesting, make people want to find out what happened? Even experienced historians ask themselves, 'How much should I focus on my subject, and how much context should I give?'

There is no simple answer to any of these questions, as it depends on your subject matter, the issues it calls you to address, and the audience you wish to reach.

Developing a structure

The chronology vs. theme tension can be approached in various ways. First, make sure you know what the chronology is. You might do this by actually writing out a narrative of the events in sequence, or perhaps simply drawing up a timeline, a shorthand summary of the order of events. This helps give a sense of development over time and, more importantly, of influences and causes. Later events cannot make earlier ones happen, so it is wise to be sure which came first.

However, it isn't as simple as developing a single timeline, for there are likely to be several parallel timelines for the story you want to tell. Furthermore, some parts of the story may cover only a few hours, or days, while other parts cover years and decades, even centuries. The timescales will vary, and you need to attune your chronology accordingly.

Next, you have to find ways to include analysis and interpretation within the narrative. Here you have many options. A sense of sequence is essential for historical understanding and explanation, but this does not mean the historian must tell a story in strict chronological order. If the narration is to live, and make analytical sense, a purely chronological framework will rarely do. Anyone who has ever written history knows that if an analysis is to be developed, strict chronology must at times be disturbed – to make different connections across time, to draw attention to contemporaneous histories, to deal with disjunctions and discontinuities. Sometimes you need, in filmic terms, a flashback. You are seeing characters at one time, but you can only understand their memories and motivations through going to an earlier period.

So you need to work out how to develop your themes and at the same time make the chronology clear. If you keep to strict chronological story-telling, you may find yourself repeating the themes with each new part of the story. On the other hand, if you organise thematically, you may find yourself zigzagging through time all over the place, so that the reader loses all sense of sequence and action.

At this point, you need a chapter plan.

Planning your chapters

If you are writing a thesis or book, and the period you are covering is reasonably long, you may wish to divide it into sub-periods. You can then discuss what happened in these sub-periods, organising your material according to theme, topic or problem. That way, you have a broad chronological structure, but have also organised much of your material thematically.

E.P. Thompson's magisterial *The Making of the English Working Class* is organised like this. The narrative moves from the late 18th century to the 1830s, but the book is in three major parts. The first looks at popular traditions influencing the Jacobin agitation of the

1790s; the second considers the impact of the industrial revolution on various groups of workers, as well as the role of Methodism in working class experience; the last part investigates working class radicalism and class consciousness.[2]

E.J. Hobsbawm also divided his enduring *The Age of Capital 1848–1875* into three parts. The first is the 'Revolutionary Prelude', dealing with the European revolutions of 1848. The second is called, rather drily, 'Developments'; as Hobsbawm explains in his preface, in this section the 'chapters are divided by themes, rather than chronologically, though the main sub-periods should be clearly discernible. These are the quiet but expansionist 1850s, the more turbulent 1860s, the boom and slump of the 1870s'. The third part, 'Results', investigates the economy, society and culture of the third quarter of the 19th century.[3]

If your work is shorter, or the period is relatively short, you might decide to stay with a single chronology, but to break your narrative from time to time to draw attention to places, contexts, ideas, parallel events, and much more. You will need to step aside from the timeline to introduce characters, or historical actors, and this will usually mean stepping back in time to give a sense of the person and who they are. Historical individuals need to be introduced properly – just as in a social situation. Moreover, the nature of your introduction will depend on whether or to what extent your intended readers already know, or know of, the person. We think it helps to introduce a person briefly, just enough for the reader to be able to see how this person fits into the story; you can then reveal more details as the narrative progresses.

Linda Colley does this in *Britons: Forging the Nation*. She first mentions one of her key figures, John Wilkes, as a campaigner for English rights, and a few lines further on tells us that he had been challenged to a duel that he avoided with 'his customary blend of wit, pomposity, impudence and intelligence'. We learn later about his chauvinism and hatred of the Scots, and much else, as the analysis demands.[4]

Whichever structure you choose – chronological, thematic, a mixture of the two – remember that chapters do not stand wholly alone. Although each deals with a discrete chunk of subject matter, the chapters in a book must connect with each other in some way to build up your sustained argument, so don't forget the overall plot.

A word or two on chapter length. Chapters don't have to be all the same length, and indeed, variation in length can sometimes be a virtue. As a general rule, however, we think chapters shouldn't be longer than 10 000 words (35 pages in double spacing). We think 8000 words (27 pages) is *much* better. If you can say what you want to say in 6000 words, better still. There are two main reasons for suggesting chapters not be too long. First, consider the reader. An 8000 word chapter is a solid chunk of reading time. You don't want your readers to lose concentration, get tired, have to get up and go somewhere, seek sustenance or go for a comfort stop before they get to the end of the chapter. The other reason is that with very long chapters it is hard to keep focused on a single strong theme or argument. Too much is going on; you are trying to keep too many balls in the air. Shorter chapters mean that you can make one strong point in each, and organise your disparate material accordingly.

A note especially to PhD students: beware of overlong chapters! There is a growing tendency for chapters to get ever longer. Work it out so that no chapter needs to be more than 8000 words. If you are writing 100 000 words you need at least twelve chapters; for 80 000 words, you need at least ten.

One way to develop your themes within an overall chronological structure is to provide sub-headings. (Some professors don't like them; in examinable pieces, check with the marker before you use them.) Sub-headings can serve a very useful purpose, indicating that you are moving onto another issue and key area for discussion, and can help you and the reader draw breath. Be careful not to fragment your chapter by using too many; keep the overall narrative coherent throughout.

Action and suspense

Get on with the action![5] Keep the story moving, and don't allow it to be bogged down in detail. Vary the pace to maintain interest, and so that it doesn't feel like just one damned thing after another.

Historians can learn from novelists and screenwriters, who think much more than we usually do about questions of plot and pace, and about developing interest and suspense. Fiction writers often speak of a 'narrative arc'. By this they mean the shape of the story – the rises and falls in tension, the high and low points, the turning points. Of course it varies according to the story being told, but a common narrative arc starts with exposition of characters and situation, develops rising tension through a series of complications and struggles facing the main characters, and comes to some kind of climax late in the story, followed by resolution.

Australian historian Alan Atkinson

I give students, say, Banjo Paterson's poem 'The Man from Snowy River', and talk to them about the way the literary/dramatic impact is due to the movement from introductory detail, to early action

> and clearing away of alternative possibilities (all the time making the reader more familiar with necessary detail), towards climax and conclusion, with the reader putting down the work at the end with a satisfied smile ... The strongest points should be left to the climax, so as to create maximum punch.

Suspense is a key element in story-telling. For your readers to care about what will happen next, two things need to happen: they need to care about the key characters (we discuss this in more detail in chapter 9), and there should be a sense of several possibilities. Because historians know the outcome, and what happened next, it is often all too easy to forget that the people at the time did not. It is actually quite difficult to convey this sense of uncertainty, to create a sense of surprise. Yet this is your task as a historian, to try to recapture that sense of *not* knowing what would happen next, to place your readers in the position of the people of the past and help them see what dilemmas they faced, and why they made the decisions they did. Try to convey this sense of options. Think of the common phrase, 'with the benefit of hindsight'. In writing narrative history, you have to make sure your hindsight, your knowledge of how things turned out, is a benefit, and not a liability deadening your prose and killing your story. The deadening effect can be especially severe if you openly narrate the past in terms of what happened later, as in 'little did he know' something or other. Phrases like these can sometimes be used well, to hint at danger or difficulty, but all too often you can end up sounding condescending and patronising.

You can still have suspense when you know the outcome. When you watch the movie *Titanic*, you know the ship will eventually sink, but there is still suspense in seeing what happens to the characters you have come to know in the course of the movie. Ann Curthoys has seen Hitchcock's *North by Northwest* a zillion times, but still feels anxious every time, near the end, when Eva Marie Saint has to escape from that house. So Hitchcock was not called the master of suspense for nothing. It's a matter of technique. Without claiming to know the secret to creating suspense, we suggest that you try writing as if you *don't* know what happened next. This is what popular historian Barbara Tuchman advocates: write, she says, '*as of the time*, without using the benefit of hindsight, resisting always the temptation to refer to events still ahead'. In describing how she wrote *The Guns of August*, about the first month of the First World War, she says, 'I wrote as if I did not know who would win'.[6]

Australian historian Geoffrey Blainey maintains suspense in *The Tyranny of Distance*, with its account of the penal settlement at Sydney Cove awaiting the arrival of ships carrying food from Britain. The small settlement was not yet self-sufficient in growing its own food: 'The weekly ration of uncooked food allowed to adults who remained in Sydney was reduced to a diet of slow starvation … Many convicts were no longer strong enough to hoe the soil vigorously, and the governor humanely accepted the fact.' After more details of the dire situation, Blainey shifts the narrative to the ships that were so late arriving in Sydney:

> While convicts in Australia crouched over iron pots on wood
> fires and boiled their salted pork and rice, a few heavily laden
> supply ships were tossing on the long sea-lane from England.
> The first relief ship did not sail from Plymouth until July 1789,
> two years and two months after the first fleet had sailed. *Lady
> Juliana*, old and leaking, carried only a small stock of provisions,
> and twenty casks of her precious flour were destroyed by sea
> water during the passage.

Finally, the *Lady Juliana* reaches Sydney Heads:

> News of her arrival was signalled from the long-idle flagstaff,
> and passed from mouth to mouth until it reached the hungry
> men hoeing hungry ground at the most distant clearing. Within
> a few days her letters and newspapers from England, and, above
> all, a little of her flour were ashore. The famine was over ...
> [By] the end of the same month four more English ships had
> entered the harbour.

Though Blainey's readers most likely know that the initial colony survived, we still share the anxiety of those officers and convicts in the tiny settlement, and feel relieved, as they did, when the ship carrying provisions finally arrives.[7]

Historians, however, can follow the fiction writers only so far. We can learn a great deal from them in terms of creating interest, tension and variation in the narrative. Perhaps we can even borrow from them a concern with story climax and resolution, by structuring each chapter and perhaps the book as a whole so that these occur near the end. We can certainly use techniques such as scene-setting, exposition and flashbacks. But there are real limits to this borrowing, for history is *not* fiction and does indeed have to obey its own rules. We cannot shape the story on purely aesthetic grounds, for there are, of course, always the sources, and the complexities of their interpretation, to deal with. As Ann Curthoys and John Docker wrote in *Is History Fiction?*, history has a double character, occupying an uncertain space between history as part of the world of literary forms and history as the rigorous scrutiny of sources. This means that history can be neither purely scientific nor purely literary. This duality lies at the heart of history's fascination for both its writers and, especially, its readers, but it also presents the historian with some serious writing challenges.

Ann Curthoys:

When writing *Freedom Ride*, I had in mind the narrative of a road movie. [8] My characters were students on a bus travelling from town to town in eastern Australia to challenge racial discrimination. I established the history of race relations of each town, in a flash back, as the bus neared that town in my narrative. In the crucial towns, the story slowed down so that one town took a whole chapter to narrate, and another took two. As the story started to become repetitive, I speeded it up, covering more towns. The most dramatic parts of the story were probably the bus being run off the road by irate whites, and then a major confrontation between the students and townsfolk in the largest town, Moree. These, however, occur in the middle third of the book, not near the end. There was still a lot of important story to tell – the later towns visited by the students, the subsequent huge public discussion, the smaller protests, and the emergence of the students' leader, Charles Perkins, as a leading spokesperson for Aboriginal rights. I added a final chapter on what happened to the freedom riders over the next thirty years. I'm not sure that I wholly succeeded, and if I were writing that book now would probably shorten it considerably, especially the first chapter. I did, though, try to keep the narrative strategies of novelists and film-makers in mind.

Point of view

You have decided how to structure your narrative. You've worked out how to manage your themes and your chronology. You have a chapter plan that seems at least a good framework for presenting your material, though you know you may have to change it as you go along. You still have a major issue to confront, however, and that is what *form* your narration will take.

One of the main reasons historians have a questionable reputation as communicators is that we too often adopt a boring narrative persona – that of the hidden narrator. A novel has a strong narrative voice, which is not that of the author as individual but of the persona the author has adopted to tell this particular story. We historians, by contrast, tend to avoid such a voice, to hide our own researches and the interventions we have made to produce a coherent credible narrative. The preface and the endnotes are exceptions, where we sometimes let ourselves go. We often don't make comments about ourselves or how we found the relevant information. We don't confide that the story in question could be interpreted in a variety of ways. We try to sound neutral – 'balanced' and disembodied. Given the traditional emphasis on trying to convey the past as it was, to make the past seem to 'speak for itself', we often believe we should not draw attention to ourselves. We rarely say 'I'.

Many historians like to continue the fiction that the past somehow directly speaks through us for itself.[9] Some advocate this approach very explicitly. Manning Clark, for example, wrote:

> Don't discuss the problems of writing with the reader; don't tell
> the reader what is happening, or comment on what is happening,
> that is don't act the role of a coach captain on a tourist bus and
> comment on the scene, but let the scene speak for itself. All the
> great stories of humankind are told without any comment at all
> … If the writer intervenes then he puts the stamp of his own
> generation on his work.[10]

In a similar vein, historian Bill Gammage talks about writing *The Broken Years*, a landmark study of the Australian experience of the tragedy of the First World War; his account of his own practice accords well with Clark's advice. He aims, he says, not to make his own intrusion as a historian obvious, and to let the story unfold as it would have seemed at the time.[11]

Yet if we like to hide behind our prose, at the same time we *do* like to sound authoritative. Think of the voice-overs in documentary films. They often choose a deep, authoritative male voice, providing a sense of omniscience – akin to the echoing-from-above all-knowing voice featured in so many classic Hollywood films. You know the type – emulating the 'voice of God' as spoken by Charlton Heston in Cecil B. de Mille's *The Ten Commandments* (1956).

French critic Roland Barthes put this style of narration under the microscope in his well-known essay 'Historical Discourse' (1967). Barthes was a structural linguist best known for heretically extending the methods of textual analysis beyond literary texts to any kind of texts – any kind of cultural or semiotic material – including even a wrestling match or a street poster.[12] In 'Historical Discourse' he made an early attempt to deconstruct the way historians' texts work. Given that historical narrative is just one particular way of viewing the world, he asked: How does it go about convincing its readers that it is the *only* way, is 'true'? The answer lay in the historian's rhetoric. In conventional historical writing, he noted, the author characteristically stands aside: there is no 'I' in the narrative. This absence is designed to produce in the reader a sense of the immediate presence of the past, and to guarantee and enhance the privileged status of history as objective knowledge. It is, Barthes felt, but a 'particular form of fiction', where the historian 'tries to give the impression that the referent is speaking for itself'.[13]

Historian and philosopher Michel Foucault also opposed the way traditional historians tried to create an objective tone in their writing, and the way they took extreme pains to 'erase the elements in their work which reveal their grounding in a particular time and place, their preferences in a controversy'. In the foundational essay 'Nietzsche,

Genealogy, History', he criticised the traditional historian's attempts to 'blur his own perspective and replace it with the fiction of a universal geometry'.[14] Such erasure places the historian in a lofty position, knowing and ironic about the consequences of actions that the historical participants could not foresee.

In the language of narrative theory, when we write this way, we are using a *third person omniscient form of narration*.[15] This is a form of story-telling in which the narrator is not a character in the story, but tells the reader about the feelings and ideas of the characters, and provides additional information unknown to them. The narrator, in fact, understands everything that happened, and tells the story in such a way that only one interpretation is possible.

Historians have found this form of narration extremely seductive, seemingly inescapable. Even when the desire to experiment with form is there, we find it extremely difficult to write in new ways. Some historians fear that history's authority and power to intervene usefully in certain venues – like the courts, the heritage tribunals, rights claims, and government policy advice – will be jeopardised by any suggestion that *what* and *how* we write is open to challenge.

While some historians manage to write engaging omniscient narrative, more often the effect is deadly dull. The historian fails to convey the excitement of history, the struggle to learn more and understand what happened in the past, and why it happened the way it did. The question is then: What other narrative points of view can historians use?

Experiment with point of view

One approach is to make ourselves visible as narrators. Inga Clendinnen admires those historians who foreground the 'struggle of the historian intent on recuperation to make the gnomic, refractory remnants of past sensibilities speak'. She wants historians to foreground those struggles in the text itself, not to bury them in footnotes.[16] In this kind of narration, the historian presents himself or herself as a detective figure attempting to work out from the (incomplete and sometimes contradictory) evidence what may have happened in the past. In *Unredeemed Captive*, for example, John Demos admits what he doesn't know and can't know from historical sources and current sensibilities.[17] He is not just detective, he is weighing up the possibilities of meaning in the sources he has. Some historians use this technique to good effect, reminding the reader that the historian, not the past itself, is telling the story. It's a form of sharing the difficult processes of discovery and interpretation.

Foregrounding the process of discovering and interpreting information about the past leads us directly to the question of the 'I' voice. For generations teachers have told history students at school and university never to use 'I' in their essays. Any student of history using the personal pronoun risked censure as self-indulgent, unscholarly, even arrogant, so that to avoid the 'I' voice became almost instinctive; to use it seemed like sacrilege.

We don't share these concerns. In our view, 'I' is okay. It all depends how you use it.

Direct personal address should not be used to circumvent the historian's task of rigorously using, and giving a fair hearing to, all the relevant sources available. History is not about simply asserting one's opinion: we always have the historical evidence to consider. Used properly, however, 'I' can often be helpful. It conveys the existence of interpretation in general and of our own interpretation in particular. We can draw attention to the possibility of other views, interpretations, and ways of representing the past, and to the limited nature of historical knowledge. By saying 'I', we leave the reader freer to judge and weigh up the historical narrative we have offered, and allow ourselves the space to admit what we do not know, or cannot figure out. The 'I' voice can help your readers understand the mediating role of the historian.

Using 'I' helps you acknowledge how personal experience and social factors shape your research goals. Indigenous and African American and Asian historians, for example, usefully build histories based on their family and personal knowledge. Other historians can learn something from this approach. In *The Sea Captain's Wife*, Martha Hodes starts off with a chapter entitled 'A Story and a History' which openly reveals her motives and methods, switching between 'I' for what she as historian has done, and the impersonal third person to present her analytical insights. Although most of the book is in the third person, in her final chapter, entitled 'Searching for Eunice', Hodes makes a switch back to an 'I' voice, narrating her research journey and reflecting upon more recent public memory around her central historical character.[18]

That said, if you do use 'I', use it sparingly. Draw the reader into dilemmas of interpretation, but only when necessary. Even if you do decide to say 'I', you'll find that you won't need to use it very often.

Multiple points of view

Another approach commonly used by novelists is the limited third-person point of view. That is, the story is witnessed through the eyes and understanding of only one person, and we, the readers, know only what that person knows. We look over that person's shoulder at everything that is happening. This kind of narration is excellent for building suspense, but it is hard for a historian to sustain for any length of time, as we do know more than one historical actor could have known, and we want to impart that knowledge. At some point, we will have to introduce other characters, other scenarios, and broaden the canvas and the point of view.

If limited third person narration is not open to us, or at least we cannot sustain it for any length of time, another way to convey the complexity of the past and of historical knowledge itself would be to use *multiple* points of view. Several narrators, each of them telling their part of the story in the first person, might tell the story. This technique is common in film. Think of Akira Kurosawa's *Rashomon*, in which a crime is described by four people who were all present, and who give completely different accounts of what happened. It is also effectively used in other formats, such as radio, television and museum displays.

In written histories, you might convey something of the same idea by constructing a number of narrative voices using letters, diaries, memoirs, anything written by a historical actor in the first person. In his celebrated 1991 essay, 'History of Events and the Revival of Narrative', British historian Peter Burke reported on and encouraged further development of this experiment in form and technique. He suggests that multi-voiced story-telling can 'allow an interpretation of conflict in terms of a conflict of interpretations'. [19]

Burke was influenced by the work of Russian cultural theorist Mikhail Bakhtin. Bakhtin distinguished between the *dialogic* and the *monologic* novel. In the former there is a play of voices, where each character represents a different troubled worldview, and where the clash of characters, and therefore of different world views, is never finalised or completed. In contrast, the monologic novel insists on one pervading set of values.[20] Burke also cites with approval Richard Price's landmark text, *Alabi's World* (1990).[21] The world referred to in the title is 18th century Saramaka, in the former Dutch colony of Suriname in northern South America, and Alabi, great-grandson of enslaved Africans, is the principal chief. In this world, various groups of people meet and interact. To narrate the encounter, Price juxtaposes four different voices, each in a different type-face. Two are taken from the first-hand documentary accounts of German-Moravian missionaries and Dutch colonial administrators, and one from the oral histories of modern Saramaks. The fourth voice is Price's own.

The use of multiple points of view in historical writing is found in collections of oral histories on a common theme. These can vary from compilations with little or no connecting narration, to works which include both lengthy oral history transcripts and the historian's commentary and narration. Recent examples of texts which are essentially compilations include *Last Line of Defence: New Zealanders Remember the War at Home, Russia's Sputnik Generation: Soviet Baby Boomers Talk about their Lives* and *Shattered Dreams? An Oral History of the South African Epidemic.*[22] A more interventionist text is Patsy Cravens' *Leavin' a Testimony: Portraits from Rural Texas.* Craven intersperses the transcripts with her own comments and introduces each of her informants. She begins one of her 89 oral history stories this way:

> 'I'm eighty-two. I'll be eighty-three on the fifteenth of October. Yes'm, hmm, hmm, and I'm preparin' for another home, 'cause you cain't have two. I'm eighty-two, and I thank the Lord I've lived such a long time, ha, hah, yes!' exclaimed Rosezena in a happy voice, 'I *thank* the Lord for my past days. And I'm preparin' every day for a better home. Yes'm, and it's time to tell my story.' These were Rosezena Woodson's words on the day we first met in 1991, when I dropped by. It was time for Rosezena to talk, and she was ready.[23]

Written histories that simply juxtapose different accounts have their limitations, however. History writers and producers primarily seek to make sense of the past – so alongside the recognition of the 'point of view' and the incompatibility of different viewpoints, it is important to recognise the reader's 'desire for truth': to know what happened. You need to decide what you think happened, and why, and convey that decision to the reader. If you don't tell them, they will assume you don't know. You may be aware that your judgment is contestable and not final, but nonetheless you need to present a strong authorial voice. There may be a complex construction of competing voices in your narrative, but in the end, people want to know what *you* think happened, and why, and how.

8

Styling pasts for presents

A scrupulous writer, in every sentence that he writes, will ask himself at least four questions, thus: 1. What am I trying to say? 2. What words will express it? 3. What image or idiom will make it clearer? 4. Is this image fresh enough to have an effect?

GEORGE ORWELL, *POLITICS AND THE ENGLISH LANGUAGE*[1]

Style: we'd all like to have it! Here we provide you with some items for your tool-kit. The nature of your prose, the often intuitive devices that shape the way it looks and sounds and makes sense to your reader: that's history's styling. Style includes voice, vocabulary, grammar, figures of speech, flow and cadence. Style is all about communication, and yet it is also something very personal. It comes from your life, and your experience as a writer. It is something quite individual, so much so that forensic linguists can identify the authors of anonymous texts from their style. While our style will change over time, we can also improve it enormously through continual practice, experimentation and reflection.

There are many excellent general advice books on writing and we don't aim to replicate them here. The bible of style, especially in the United States, is probably William Strunk and E.G. White's *The Elements of Style*.[2] Also very popular is William Knowlton Zinsser's *On Writing Well: The Classic Guide to Writing Nonfiction*. Mark Tredinnick's *The Little Red Writing* Book is a more recent favourite.[3] Read them, and use them when you write. Here, we concentrate on some style issues that historians in particular need to confront when they write.

Voice

Good writers often sound as though they are talking to you. Some are witty; some are full of empathy. Some offer clear, strong views. Others are just wonderful storytellers. Great writers can be brilliantly succinct.

Many writers, including many historians, get stuck trying to find the right 'voice'. What is the right voice? It's the voice that flows, that allows you to proceed into a relaxed and useful conversation with your audience. Why haven't you found it? Perhaps you are trying to write like someone else. Perhaps you have a preconceived idea of what 'a historian' *should* sound like. In trying to sound earnest, reliable, serious and sincere, some people can end up sounding pompous and pretentious, others bland and dull. If this is the problem, consider lightening up a bit.

In reading historians who have found their own voice, you can hear them in your ears, and see the images they paint before your eyes. It is no effort to read good writing in a strong and 'true' voice. Rather, it is easy listening; it is enjoyable; it flows, and you flow along with it.

The elements of prose

Let's now look at some of the basics of writing.

Paragraphs

Paragraphs break your writing into manageable sections, and help you move through your ideas. Use paragraphs to indicate a shift in the narration, the argument, or perhaps the tone. The first sentence, called the 'topic sentence', should introduce the topic of the paragraph, and what follows should all 'belong'. Paragraphs are best kept fairly short. Don't let a paragraph expand into a whole page of double spacing. Break your paragraphs up into ideas – smallish ideas. The breaks give the reader a little bit of eye relaxation, a bit of time to await the next thought. They indicate a conceptual pause, a moment – or several moments.

Tense

Perhaps you are wondering why historians would stress about tense. Surely the one thing we know about history is that it resides in the house of the past tense. But not necessarily – let's experiment. Present tense can sometimes bring a dramatised sense of immediacy. It can allow the reader to imagine something is happening now, lending a freshness, a 'being there' sense to the narrative. Think of watching a historical play or film; despite their subject's pastness, they are performed or 'told' in the present tense. Historian Greg Dening, drawing upon theatrical thinking, entitled a major study of historical writing *Performances*.[4] His advice was: be mysterious, be experiential, be compassionate, be entertaining, and be performative. Keen to 'return to the past its own present', in a later essay Dening applied the present tense to describe the death of Gauguin through the artist's own eyes; he allows us to see what Gauguin saw from his sickbed:

Gauguin cannot stand at his easel any more. The pain in his ulcerated legs is too great even with the morphine. He is breathless with angina. His syphilis is taking away his eyesight. His eyes look piggy behind the steel rimmed circles of his spectacles. He knows he will not paint for much longer. He knows he is dying. His last painting has a realism his others don't possess. He paints himself as [a] dead man walking.[5]

As the clipped drama of these short sentences suggests, Dening liked to read his prose aloud, experiencing his own words aloud, and its impact on the audience.

Generally, the best advice about tense is to keep it consistent. You can't chop and change tenses within the same paragraph. Make sure the tense enhances the sharpness of your meaning around events, order and timing. If you choose to try the present tense to achieve the fresh 'it's happening now' narrative style, signal when you drop it again. In general, it is difficult to sustain for any length of time.

Sentences

Remember grammar lessons? Subject, verb, predicate? Some of you will, some of you won't, as grammar became deeply unfashionable and was largely omitted from the school curriculum. We include here some basics; if you need more, Mark Tredinnick's *Little Green Grammar Book* may come in helpful.[6] Most grammar is about constructing clear and meaningful sentences.

Sentences normally have a subject, a verb and an object. Occasionally you can write a verbless or subjectless sentence, but only for impact, for rhythm or pace, and not too frequently. Rhythm, pace – impact. Favour shorter sentences wherever possible. Sentences with more than three clauses can force the reader to reread them to discern the sense of the whole. Check for sentences longer than five lines and consider breaking them into two or more sentences.

This is from a 1993 essay by the American frontier historian, Patricia Nelson Limerick, entitled 'Dancing with Professors'. (The title is drawn from her memory that professors were the ones that nobody wanted to dance with at school.) Limerick created a hypothetical account of an encounter between academic writer and reader. When the reader admits to not understanding what they are reading, the academic writer responds: 'Too bad. The problem is that you are an unsophisticated and untrained reader. If you were smarter, you would understand me.'

Limerick stridently objects to this kind of snobbery, railing especially against over-long sentences crammed with too many ideas:

In their company, one starts to get panicky. 'Throw open the windows; bring in the oxygen tanks!' one wants to shout. 'These words and ideas are nearly suffocated. Get them air!'...

[E]veryone knows that today's college students cannot write, but few seem willing to admit that the professors who denounce them are not doing much better. The problem is so blatant that there are signs that the students are catching on. In my American history survey course last semester, I presented a few writing rules that I intended to enforce inflexibly. The students looked more and more peevish; they looked as if they were about to run down the hall, find a telephone, place an urgent call and demand that someone from the A.C.L.U. rush up to campus to sue me for interfering with their First Amendment rights to compose unintelligible, misshapen sentences.

Finally one aggrieved student raised her hand and said, 'You are telling us not to write long, dull sentences, but most of our reading is full of long, dull sentences.'[7]

Some people think they lose the links between ideas when they break up sentences. Introductory words like 'then', 'therefore', 'after which', and the inclusion of 'thus' and 'however' can assist in suggesting a flow of logic. Using 'but' or 'and' at the beginning of a sentence is grammatically incorrect, according to most grammar teachers. But Ann McGrath often likes it. Occasionally one can be a grammar rebel. Very often, though, the link is implied, and you don't have to worry.

Rhythm

Read your prose aloud, hear how it sounds. Does it flow, sound pleasing and/or exciting? Is it pacey and exhilarating? Or does it sound boring, monotonous, dull? Do you find yourself stumbling over the words and phrases, barely able to sustain enough breath to get to the end of ridiculously over-long sentences? Learn from some of the greatest exponents of history writing, like Thomas Macaulay:

> Of the many errors which James committed, none was more fatal
> than this. Already he had alienated the hearts of his people by
> violating their laws, confiscating their estates, and persecuting their
> religion. Of those who had once been most zealous for monarchy,
> he had already made many rebels in heart.[8]

The fluency of a text, the pleasure in the way the words rise and fall, isn't important only because of the aesthetic pleasure of reading it. It's also an indication of clarity of thought and the strength of the connections between the various parts of a sentence, a paragraph, a chapter.

Words

Get the word just right. Is there a better one? Avoid obscure or very long words not in common usage. If you need to use such a word, define it clearly within your sentence or the next sentence.

One of your favoured styling tools should be a dictionary. If you are one of the few who don't like opening a book with hard covers, you can find one online. Dictionaries can inspire you with more of the meanings in words and their history, as well as interesting alternatives. If you have any doubt about a word, if it looks odd or sounds strange, look it up. Maybe it seems like a nice solid word, but it turns to mud in the wrong company. Ditch it and use it another time.

Choose your language to fit your audience. You can use more specialised language in a scholarly monograph or journal than you can in a popular book or newspaper article. If you do need to use a word unfamiliar to your audience, be sure to explain it clearly. When a new generation of historians took up postmodern theory from the 1980s, established scholars worried about the very essence of their discipline being lost in gobbledygook. And sometimes that certainly happened. The truth is that new language and conceptual frameworks can jolt, provoke, and allow new interpretations. You need not avoid theory, or new and unfamiliar concepts, but you must ensure they are presented in a way that is comprehensible to the reader.

LANGUAGE DON'TS

REPETITION

Never say anything twice. Even if both times you say things really quite beautifully and differently, never say anything twice. Well, that was kind of pointedly said twice. Always exceptions! Sometimes, repetition helps you make a point, and it's a favoured technique in public rhetoric. Think of President Obama's wonderful use of repetition in his speeches. In historical writing, though, repetition, even when obscured by some other prose in between, usually makes your exposition tedious.

Don't get stuck overusing a much-loved word. A word like 'imbricated' or even 'linked' can become an excuse for poor discussion of causation. A favoured word like 'intervention' can lose meaning with over-use. Also, 'also' can become a little tedious after a while.

PRONOUNS

Don't allow your character to be lost in a pronoun. With other points intervening, a 'he' that is obvious to the author may be lost to oblivion to the reader.

Avoid 'one'. That kind of distancing is now way too old-fashioned for history writing. Sometimes it works okay, perhaps (see if you can find where we used it in this chapter) but don't let the neutralised, passively regenerating 'one' multiply into plague proportions. It is much better to use 'I', 'he' or 'she'. Because 'he' and 'she' present problems when you want to be gender neutral, you can opt for 'they', but don't forget your matching plural verbs. Another option, which we use in this book, is 'you'.

SINGULAR AND PLURAL

Don't get your plurals and singulars mixed up. They are especially easy to mess you up if your subject is lost in long, multi-clause sentences. 'This tedious group of monarchs were ostentatious.' No, the group *was* ostentatious. This kind of singular term for more than one will trick you into thinking it is plural, but no, the monarchs *were* ostentatious; the group *was*. Having said that, 'this tedious group of monarchs was ostentatious' sounds pretty weird to us. It's much better to rearrange the sentence than to end up with awkward and pedantic formulations. Just say 'These tedious monarchs were ostentatious'.

CLARITY

Don't be vague. Sometimes referring to 'the latter' can be confusing – why not just indicate the clause or option to which you refer?

TRUNCATIONS

Truncations are a no-no, except in speech. Yes, we've used 'don't' and 'can't' and other abbreviations to create an informal, conversational style – but this is a history guide book, not a formal history text.

EXCLAMATION MARK

Use the exclamation mark only in speech. If a point is worth making, it doesn't need an exclamation mark to emphasise it. (Occasionally it can be used to indicate humour. If you are making a comment that is meant to be taken lightheartedly, an exclamation mark can assist the reader to recognise this.)

Use present-day language

Write in present-day language, not the language of the period you are writing about. Admirable though it is, the ideal of writing about the people of the past 'in their own terms' rather than ours *sounds* respectful, but it can lead to a failure to connect with your current audience. The result is prose that is dead on the page.

Resist the temptation to mimic the language and phrasing of the period. (It's also very difficult to keep it up with any degree of authenticity and consistency.) While you may have conscientiously immersed yourself in your historical sources, and absorbed the terminology of the day, its special style of language and even the rhythm of its prose, most readers will not be as keen as you are. The stilted tone of archival files or the outmoded prose laden with the undiagnosed 'weasel words' of bureaucratic speak can lead to tedium.[9] Mimicry is not only unappealing to current readers, but can lead you to replicate – rather than analyse – contemporary assumptions from the period under review. Your job is not to emulate the language of the past, its values or its precepts, but to expose its uniqueness, to explore and demonstrate the differences between that past and the present. Deconstruct rather than rehearse contemporary language. It's a little like being a good cross-cultural practitioner.

However, while you are decoding language, don't lose the *immediacy* of the time that its different-sounding language and encoded conceptualisations can reveal. Retaining the flavour of the language through quotations is an important storytelling device. (We discuss quotations in more detail in chapter 9.) Phrases or a few sentences will be enough to give the flavour of the language of your historical actors.

Translate uncommon or obsolete words into modern language. Many people will not know what a *shabunder* is, or a *shabraque*, a *shaveling*, a *slibbersauce* or a *socage*, so if you need to use such words, explain their meaning. The reader needs your help here.

Terminology

All scholars want to get their terminology right – accurate, meaningful, and not offensive. Historians face some particular problems arising from the differences between current and past usages. We discussed the interpretation of the language of historical documents in chapter 3; here we consider how these issues affect your own writing.

What do you do when a term, now considered derogatory by certain groups, was generally accepted during the relevant historical period? Today the word might have sexual or racist overtones, might insult a whole nationality or religion. Its derogatory nature

STYLE DO'S and DON'TS

DO'S

DO write in present-day language; literate medievals are not your readers.

DO quote from past documents to give the flavour of how people wrote and spoke in the past; peppering your writing with contemporary phrases can explain different ways of thinking and thus connect the reader with past worlds.

DO distinguish your rhetoric from historical rhetoric: 'The town's local youth detested the boy who'd stolen their beautiful Natalie.' Is this a beat-up by the local press or do you have evidence that the local youth actually thought this? Is the word 'stolen' yours or theirs; whose rhetoric are we dealing with?

DO explain obsolete words.

DO read your work aloud to check that your words, phrases, clauses and sentences flow.

DO write mainly in the active voice.

DO vary the length of your sentences and paragraphs.

DON'TS

DON'T use dates as actors: '1492 saw the beginning of a new era about to envelop the world'; '1956 saw Elvis Presley having yet another lavish but happy birthday'.

DON'T use eras as actors. 'The French revolution stood overlooking the trajectory of an age imbricated with change.' Stuffy, pretentious, horrid and meaningless to boot. 'The Early Republic presided over a people obsessed with their own self-importance.' Who? What? Avoid triteness, truisms and silly nonsense.

> **DON'T** overdo 'ironically' and 'paradoxically' as sentence-starters.
>
> **DON'T** use a tone of inevitability or all-knowingness. Don't start sentences with 'Inevitably', 'It was inevitable that ...', 'Of course ...', 'Undoubtedly ...', 'Doubtless ...', 'Obviously ...', 'It was no surprise that ...', 'It goes without saying that ...', 'Needless to say ...'.
>
> **DON'T** over-generalise. For example: 'The community believed a giant green monster was about to sink all their boats.' How do you know that? Or was it certain sections of the community? Terms like 'community' suggest a homogeneity that may not be warranted.

might have evolved in the decades in between now and then. It may have been a neutral descriptor or even a respectful term during the historical period under study. Do you use the contemporary word that now sounds offensive, or switch to one more palatable today? This is worth considering carefully, because historians must confront history head-on. While we don't want to fall into the trap of omitting or smoothing over its less palatable realities, do you really want to insult and offend today's readers? Additionally, don't introduce historical anachronisms by reading insult into something not derogatory at the time.

For example, the term 'sheila' was derogatory in 1970s Australia, whereas in the late 19th century it was a term of endearment for Irish Australian girls. In the early 20th century in many countries, children born of parents from different ethnic groups were called 'hybrids', 'half-castes', 'mulattoes' and even 'quadroons'. Such race-based classification is very distasteful today and, indeed, was usually racist in its time. In some contemporary contexts, however, the terms were used to argue for superior qualities such as 'hybrid vigour' (today used only in reference to cross-bred animals and plants), involving high intelligence and improved physical qualities. Historically, people described in such terms sometimes willingly embraced them in order to differentiate themselves from other groups and to gain rights. While the word 'nigger', for example, may be used self-reflexively in rap music and other cultural settings, an author must carefully contextualize its use in historical writing. Even with the most sensitive explanation, derogatory terms like this can remain offensive.

You will notice a whole lot of quotation marks above; they draw a geographical boundary around these words, indicating they don't belong to your present-day authorial speech. Too many inverted commas can become very tedious, so it's worth using them just for the now-antiquated term's initial appearance, and explaining (in a footnote perhaps) that you will not use them for every subsequent appearance. (The same principle applies to the over-use of *italics*.)

When you are using quotations, it's a different story. If you think it important to quote directly, to impart the flavour of a person or accuracy about the period's thinking (however offensive that is to today's readers), you need to do so carefully. It is probably a good idea to explain what you've decided to do and why, either in your introduction or in a footnote. Robin W. Winks does this in the second edition of his book, *The Blacks in Canada: A History*, first published in 1971. It was republished in 1997 with a new preface, in which Winks explains that when he was researching the book in the 1960s, African-Canadians preferred to be called Negroes or coloureds, and the terms occurred repeatedly in the interviews he conducted. By the time the book was in press, terminology was changing, preferring 'blacks' to 'Negroes' and 'coloureds'. It was too late to change the text, but Winks insisted on the title *The Blacks in Canada*.[10]

Some terms may not be offensive as much as inappropriate. For example, are you using terms like 'Asians', 'Africans', 'Europeans', 'whites'? Depending on your topic, they may be general and misleading. Think carefully how you use 'civilisation' and 'race'.

While some terms may in certain contexts be in common usage, make sure you are precise about what you mean by them, especially if they are integral to your theme. History is a practice that does not take words for granted. It probes terminology; it coins new word usages and analyses the chosen words of others – all the time using words to do so. Don't let this scary thought hold you back. Get the words out now or you will have to keep revising them, re-tuning them to a new era and new ears.

Against backgrounds

Think about the parts of your writing you've relegated to 'background'. We generally hate the sections in public documents called 'Historical Background'. This heading defines them as irrelevant, as 'backdrop' – a section you don't need to read, as it is not the real stuff, not the argument, and not why you're there reading. The very term 'background' suggests the real stuff follows. In some books and official reports, this section's presence undermines the relevance and significance of the historical section.

Ann McGrath remembers painting portraits in an art class, and her teacher saying: 'Make sure every part of the painting is just as interesting as the rest.' You may have done a brilliant portrait of someone's face. So why is the background some static lifeless colour? Each part has to draw the viewer in, has to intrigue and work to the eye. No single part can let the other parts down.

In other words, there is no such thing as an obligatory 'background section'. We can learn by looking at portraits. See how the artist uses the background to make the rest work. See what they do with it, taking equal care, adding as much energy and originality to the treatment. Perhaps one section of your writing really *is* tone-setting and providing essential context. It is still part of the story. Let it live. Let it be fun. Let it pull the reader in so that they are begging for more. *Encore! Encore!*

Active and passive voice

Active voice happens when the subject of the sentence is the doer of the action: 'The Vikings attacked the monastery of Lindisfarne in about 793 AD.' In this case, the subject of the sentence is 'The Vikings', and they are the actors, the people who did something.

In a sentence written in the passive voice (like this one), the subject of the sentence is acted upon: 'The monastery of Lindisfarne was attacked by Vikings in about 793 AD.' In this case, the subject of the sentence is 'the monastery of Lindisfarne', and the monastery is not an actor; it is something acted on by others. In this sentence, the Vikings are still the doers, but they are no longer centre stage.

Sometimes the agent is not specified: 'Attacks on the monastery of Lindisfarne occurred around 793 AD.' Here, the monastery is acted on by others, but the agents of the action are not named. We don't know who they were.

The first sentence is the easiest to read, and the third is much less informative than the other two. Sentences of the second and third kind are very common in history texts. Passive-voiced historical prose often leaves the agent of the action unclear, or shifts agency from individuals and social groups to vague social processes. Using the active voice forces you to specify wherever possible *who* carried out the action, and thus it provides essential information. Where the dull hum of the passive voice makes history feel passé, the active voice enlivens it, lending a sense of immediacy, of lived action and lived lives.

The question of active and passive voice is no minor matter. Overuse of the passive construction is one of the most serious faults in historical writing. In the early drafts of chapters of history PhDs, one of the main problems we find is excessive use of the passive voice. But the over-users of the passive voice are not only PhD students – they include many professional historians. We often use this technique to avoid admitting we don't know when or why something happened or who was responsible. Such corner-cutting in your research, or hiding what you don't or can't know, has serious side-effects. Passive voice can deaden the tone and obscure meaning. Indeed, long passive-voice sentences often lose their sense altogether.

Furthermore, the question of active and passive voice goes to the heart of how we narrate, analyse and interpret what happened in the past. In a practical way, it raises the questions of agency and structure – key issues in historical interpretation. During the 1960s and 1970s, structuralist approaches to history were popular, though they always had their critics. The writers of these histories were influenced either by Marx or by social scientists more generally. In the late 1980s, many historians turned away from the structuralist approach, and became increasingly interested in agency and contingency. In women's history and postcolonial history, for example, historians stopped emphasising the structural determinants of what happened to women and indigenous peoples as subject social groups. They started to emphasise their choices, their agency and their own perspectives, desires and subjectivity, as groups and as individuals.

Turning a sentence from passive to active voice forces us to think about and specify agency. There are some occasions, however, when the passive voice might be used for good reason. We just did it – albeit for no particularly good reason. You might use the passive voice for variety, as substantial pieces of writing entirely in active voice prose become a little monotonous. You might use it to emphasise the structural determinants of action rather than individual or group agency. Or because you simply cannot specify who the agent is, and do not want to interrupt the narrative or argument with an explanatory aside. And sometimes because the name of the agent is unimportant.

Consider these sentences from that excellent prose stylist and major English historian, E.P. Thompson. He is discussing Methodism in early 19th century England:

> Methodist preachers perfected techniques to arouse paroxysms of fear of death and of the unlimited pains of Hell. Children, from the age that they could speak, were terrified with images of everlasting punishment for the slightest misbehaviour. Their nights were made lurid by Foxe's *Book of Martyrs* and similar reading.[11]

The mix of active and passive voice gives variety to the writing.

The minute you stop thinking about it, you can start to over-use passive voice in academic prose. One way to check whether your writing is active or passive is to set your computer's spell and grammar checker so that it also covers 'style'. Even in drafting this book, the number of our own passive voice sentences astonished us. We then set out to make as many as we could active, though we didn't change them all, for the reasons given above.

Metaphor for historians

Many writers of history books have difficulty in recognising the metaphoric nature of their language. They are usually surprised to be reminded how metaphoric even the everyday language of history texts actually is.

We take from literary criticism an approach that sees metaphor as always a point of ambiguity and ambivalence, potentially unhinging any statement and disturbing any grounds of certainty. A metaphor is always involved in a history of metaphors.[12] When a reader sees a metaphor in a text, say a mountain, they think of all the other places and texts (poems, novels, paintings) where mountains are riddled with teasingly diverse, perhaps contradictory meanings. An image of one mountain leads to images of other mountains, or to related images (mountain as castle of Gothic fear, or as breast, or as carnival image of plenty, or as otherworldly retreat) in an unstoppable series of images. Visual signs can be replete with complex meanings. Take a national flag – think of your own. It can signify quite different meanings in different contexts and during eras with different preoccupations: civil war, peace, soldiers at war, xenophobic nationalism. Think of the Confederate flag and the Eureka flag, with their multiple, ever-changing and contested meanings. Words can be the same.

Not only literature but also works of scholarship in the human and social sciences – philosophy, history, political science, and so forth – are suffused with metaphor. Three major 20th century philosophers of language, Walter Benjamin, Jacques Derrida and Paul de Man, all questioned the alleged purity of concepts. This 'purity', supposedly the basis of western knowledge conceived as objective and scientific, underlines claims for the superiority of western thought. It is, these philosophers suggested, a fantasy; for concepts are inevitably metaphoric and hence, to some degree, unstable.

Historical writing, like philosophical writing, is always revealingly metaphoric. Marxist histories, for example, abound in building tropes: foundation, base, superstructure, concrete (as in concrete reality or sometimes concrete foundations), material and construction. Marxists also like tropes from physics: forces, forms, motor, vector, articulation. In the 1970s and 1980s, under the influence of the Marxist philosopher Louis Althusser, metaphors became quite surgical – suture, insertion – and sometimes geological, as in the repeated use of terms such as terrain, site, level, layers, conjuncture, formation.[13] For the structuralists the tropes might be geometric: surface, deep structure, centre and 'underlying reality'. Postcolonial theorists energetically took up geographical metaphors: boundaries, travelling, nomad, lines of flight, liminality, dispersal and trace.

Traditional historians' use of metaphor has been explored by a number of authors. Anthony Easthope subjected a historical essay by Lawrence Stone to detailed literary analysis, drawing attention to the metaphoricity of Stone's text, its representation of society as a machine, and the repeated opposition it constructs between the solid and the liquid. Easthope argues that Stone's text is typical of much English historical writing, presenting itself as purely transcribing the 'obviously real', all the while employing figurative language.[14] We can think of many metaphoric terms that historians use all the time: birth of a nation, birth of an era, dawn of time, and founding father.

Innumerable metaphors have become part of everyday language, so that we don't notice their metaphoric reference: illuminate, elucidate, digest, in a fog, recipe, architecture. This is true of the words and concepts historians use all the time. Take, for example, terms like 'document' – that which teaches and instructs; 'source' – suggesting the springs from which a river begins to flow, a fluid origin; and 'evidence' – a visual metaphor indicating something from the vanished past which is brought back into sight.[15]

In *The Gender of History*, Bonnie Smith points to the value of metaphor, suggesting that metaphorical thinking has helped scientists to reconceptualise problems, make breakthroughs and nourish the formulation of new ideas. Metaphors are frequently present in scientific conceptions of matter, world and universe – as in rays, waves, the Big Bang, vectors. Metaphors are important in opening the way to new knowledge by allowing people to approach conventional problems in science in new ways; in scientific writing, metaphor is not just decorative, it is pertinent to cognition, understanding, and explanation.[16]

Because metaphors are inescapably and inevitably at work in historical writing, you need to be as self-conscious, self-reflexive and as aware as you can be of the metaphors you use. Welcome them, and create them with pleasure and exuberance for your readers. The human brain finds metaphors pleasurable; it appreciates their explanatory power. Metaphors can link abstract thinking with sensory experience. They can help the brain freshly associate the familiar with the unfamiliar, or associate the previously unassociated.

Here's an example of a striking use of metaphor, from the introduction to Richard White's *The Middle Ground*:

> The history of Indian-white relations has not usually produced complex histories. The Indians are the rock, European peoples are the sea, and history seems a constant storm. There have been but two outcomes: The sea wears down and dissolves the rock; or the sea erodes the rock but cannot finally absorb its battered remnant, which endures. The first outcome produces stories of conquest and assimilation; the second produces stories of cultural persistence. The tellers of such stories do not lie. Some Indian groups did disappear; others did persist. But the tellers of such stories miss a larger process and a larger truth. The meeting of sea and continent, like the meeting of whites and Indians, creates as well as destroys. Contact was not a battle of primal forces in which only one could survive. Something new could appear.[17]

Metaphors don't always work. Mixed metaphors jam two or more metaphors into a paragraph or a sentence so that neither has a chance of working.

The more you think about style, and check your own prose for clarity, flow, rhythm, and colour, the better your writing will be.

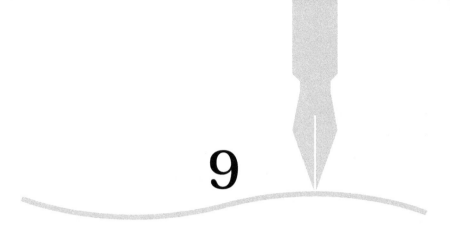

9

Character and emotion

The perfect historian is he in whose work the character and spirit of an age is exhibited in miniature. He relates no fact, he attributes no expression to his characters, which is not authenticated by sufficient testimony. But by judicious selection, rejection and arrangement he gives to truth those attractions which have been usurped by fiction.

THOMAS BABINGTON MACAULAY, 'ON HISTORY'[1]

History is filled with people doing things. These may be ordinary everyday activities or the unusual actions which precipitate major political events, wars and revolutions. For any historian, it's important to portray the people of the past so that they, and what they thought and did, matter to the reader. This is especially true in the many forms of life-writing, including biography, that prosper today, but it's also true in history more generally. This chapter considers questions such as: How can we write about the individual people of the past? How much can we understand, and what can we never know? How can we make our historical actors come alive on the page? What did the people of the past feel and believe? What did the world look like to them, and how did they look to each other? Can and should we make moral judgments about them or their actions?

Understanding past emotions

Try to explain people's ideas, motivations, desires, aspirations, emotional states and the ways others saw them. Where the sources allow, you can show how people conflicted with one another and how their disagreements played out in action, and when they agreed, made common cause, were in harmony with one another. You can use letters, diaries, memoirs and other written pieces, along with artefacts, paintings and domestic interiors to help you build a picture of the point of view of your historical actors.

We just wrote 'where the sources allow'. Hereby hangs a huge problem. What *do* the sources allow? As we indicated in the Introduction, novelists and popular writers sometimes claim that professional historians cannot present emotion and inner feelings at all. This is a serious charge that many historians reject, but it's worth a closer look.

Novelists, who can use sources as they please, have much flexibility to create complex characters that somehow make sense to us, the readers. Perhaps they introduce us to new people whom we feel they have allowed us to know. Or perhaps they are like people we actually *do* know. The novelist's characterisations enable us to imagine the way people moved, dressed and spoke. Their stories and the incidents their characters experience move us emotionally.

Historians very often do not have the sources that enable them to do this. We only have bits and pieces of evidence. Frustration at the paucity of the sources has sparked many a historical fiction book:

the writer has learnt just so much from the historical evidence, but can go no further. Whole sections of a life, or a correspondence, or a diary are missing. Itching to fill in the gaps, the writer thus turns from history to fiction. In his historical novel, *Dancing in the Dark*, based on the life of Bert Williams, the Caribbean-born American minstrel performer, English writer Caryl Phillips imagines Williams' inner turmoil. Yet the sources that tell how Bert felt about his profession and how he experienced public perception of his work do not exist.

Kate Grenville's novel, *The Secret River* (2005), has generated some lively discussion on the question of novelists, historians and the presentation of emotion. The novel started as a history of Kate's forebears as early Australian settlers and of their relations with the Aboriginal occupants of that land, but she ended up converting it to a novel, a process she describes in some detail in her follow-up text, *Searching for the Secret River*.[2] The book dealt with the very same issues that were then the subject of bitter controversy amongst historians, that is, the degree of violence and death experienced by Indigenous people during the processes of their dispossession, displacement, and replacement by British settlers. While the conservative ire against the historians who narrated these events was often vicious, not so in this case. Despite its plotlines of destruction and tragedy, the popularity of *The Secret River* seems to suggest that novelists could address difficult issues more easily than historians, and make them comprehensible to a broader audience. Grenville contrasted the historians' labours and interpretive conflicts with the novelists who could stand apart from all that and get to the heart of the matter. She said:

> I think the historians, and rightly so, have battled away about
> the details ... I think that's what historians ought to be doing;

constantly questioning the evidence and perhaps even each other
… but let me as a novelist come to it in a different way, which is
the way of empathising and imaginative understanding of those
difficult events. Basically to think, well, what would I have done in
that situation, and what sort of a person would that make me?[3]

Several historians, including Mark McKenna and Inga Clendinnen,
responded angrily to what they saw as Grenville's lofty claim that
she could write better history than they could, through a novelist's
use of imaginative understanding.[4] Others like John Hirst accused
her of failing to recognise how different the past is from the present.[5]
Grenville replied that she had been misunderstood: she did not at all
regard her book as history, and made no claims to write history. Yet
in *Searching for the Secret River*, where she describes in interesting
detail the process of *The Secret River*'s transition from non-fiction
to novel, she still claimed historical truth for her book after its
transformation into fiction:

This wasn't quite how it was in the documents, but making a
sequence out of these scenes wouldn't distort what had 'really
happened' in any significant way. It would, though, turn them
into a story.[6]

And again, a few pages later:

I was trying to be faithful to the shape of the historical record, and the
meaning of all those events that historians had written about. What I
was writing wasn't real, but it was as true as I could make it.[7]

While in some ways confusing and unresolved, the debate raised an
important issue – the degree to which historians can convey empathy
and imaginative understanding. We think they can, but there are
some serious limits.

If you want to stay with history, you won't have the same kind of freedom as the historical novelist. You can't fill in the gaps the way a novelist can. You might want to speculate, but if you do, make it clear you *are* speculating – and do not invent. Do not speculate and then write as if people *must* have experienced life this way, as if there can be no doubt that this is how they felt. In *The Sea Captain's Wife*, Martha Hodes aims for both narrativity and historical integrity and generally achieves them admirably. We question, though, her use of speculation. She writes:

> The first letters from New England arrived in Cayman two and a half years after Eunice's departure. Those pages haven't survived, but surely they were filled with recountings of the family's whereabouts, health, and various endeavors, along with news of the New England economy and Reconstruction politics. No doubt the letters reassured Eunice how much everyone (or almost everyone) missed her and the children, and no doubt they contained regards for Smiley and his kin.[8]

Although Hodes' language creates an aura of integrity and reliability, her use of qualifiers such as 'no doubt' and 'surely' is something of a false caution. If there's 'no doubt', why use the expression at all? Perhaps 'perhaps' would have been more appropriate, and truer to the historian's obligation to the historical record.

The problems facing historians who want to evoke character and emotion are not just those arising from a lack of sources. Sometimes the sources are there, but what do you make of them? Although your historical subjects share with you a common humanity, a hugely important facet of history-writing, in other ways they are not like you at all. They are somewhat strange. Their emotions may have been quite different from yours, thus imagining what they might have felt could lead you in the wrong direction. You cannot assume that something that makes us angry or sad or happy or amused did the same for them. Cultural historian Robert Darnton built a whole essay, 'The Great Cat Massacre', around the observation that what made some 18th century shop apprentices in Paris laugh hilariously, the killing of large numbers of cats, we no longer find funny.[9] American feminist historian Joan Scott has also pointed out that we cannot assume we know the emotions and felt experiences of women or men of the past; rather, we need to understand the ways in which experience has changed over time, and has been historically constituted.[10]

In one common field of historical study, that of first or early contact between peoples, often indigenous peoples and Europeans, you need to be particularly wary. You might wonder about how indigenous peoples reacted when they first met Europeans, and you can note (as far as the largely European sources allow) what they did, but you should not present your speculations on their thoughts as historical reality. You need to read the European accounts of first contact in the context of European assumptions and be suspicious of their understandings of indigenous peoples. You have to allow sometimes that your sources simply do not enable you to achieve this kind of understanding.

This is difficult territory. You want to respect your sources and not invent. Yet you also want to move your readers, to help them understand how people thought and felt in the past. You want to engage their emotions and sympathies, want them to care about the story you are telling. After all, people in the past had emotions, and to write as if they didn't is misleading. Australian historian of manners Penny Russell adeptly puts the case for writing about past people's emotions:

> The emotional landscape of our subjects is buried with the dust of their living, feeling bodies. What lingers is our own capacity for a feeling response to the words they wrote when living. … We need to reach and move our readers: not to reactive moral judgments, nor to sentimental endorsement of the actions of the past, but to something approaching historical understanding.[11]

One way through the dilemma of how to understand and represent past emotions might be to focus on the differences between then and now. By investigating in depth why his 18th century shop apprentices in Paris enjoyed the killing of cats, Robert Darnton was able to explore their world view, their lives in context, and at the same time to contribute to our understanding of the history of emotions. As Darnton put it, 'By getting the joke of the great cat massacre, it may be possible to "get" a basic ingredient of artisan culture under the Old Regime.'[12]

Alternatively, you can think how *you* might have reacted, and then look more closely at the sources to see whether there is any indication that that was indeed how people reacted at the time. Use your own experience as a starting point, but realise that is all it is. As we build up our knowledge of the history of emotions, we can better understand how people's emotions changed in nature and intensity over time.[13]

The five senses: sight, sound, smell, taste, and touch

Ask yourself: What did my protagonists see, smell and hear? The answers may help you provide background, or they might assist you with key matters of causation. Thinking of the five senses will help you remember that history happened to human beings. It will help you think yourself into the picture, to imagine what you would have thought, felt or done.

Be aware that the five senses are experienced differently across time and culture. What people ate in ancient Rome or Imperial China may not appeal today. With very different hygiene practices, people and their environments usually smelt different. The Jorvik Viking Centre museum in York has reproduced what may have been the smells of a Viking village in northern England in the Middle Ages, and to our noses they are strong smells.

The sounds we hear daily have changed, and keep changing. Ann McGrath was working on a study about Cornwall, Connecticut in the 1820s, when she came across a reference in a young woman's private letters to a church bell tolling. Only after thinking about it for some time did Ann realise that this was probably the loudest sound anyone would hear in that small village. There were no trucks, no planes, trains or heavy metal music. Few were authorised to ring the bell, which was only used on particular occasions – usually on 'the passing of a soul'. She wondered whether the bell almost *became* the sound of the soul passing.

We don't know much as about what people heard, smelt, tasted and touched as we would like, but historians are working on it. After the fading of the linguistic turn of the 1980s and 1990s, some have proclaimed a 'sensory turn' in historical scholarship. Look for the relevant literature to help you get an idea for your place and period, in the work of people like Constance Classen, David Howes, Robert Jutte and Mark Smith.[14]

Understanding and evoking character

All these issues – the treatment of character, emotions and the senses – take on a special intensity in the various forms of life-writing. Life-writing includes biography, autobiography, testimony and memoir, any form of writing in which there is a focus on an individual life, or part of a life. It is a growing and extremely popular form.

Probably the most popular form of history is biography. There are said to be over 10 000 biographies of Abraham Lincoln, and there are innumerable biographies of other major figures – political, military, artistic and intellectual. Historians, it seems, love to write biographies, and if the person is interesting and important enough and the biography is engaging and well written, people love to read them. This has been the case for a long time, and shows no sign of diminishing. Historian Thomas Macaulay noted in 1828, in the essay from which we took the epigraph to this chapter, that biographies like Voltaire's *Charles the Twelfth* and Boswell's *Life of Johnson* sold wonderfully well. 'Whenever any tolerable book of the same description,' he wrote, 'makes its appearance, the circulating libraries are mobbed; the book societies are in commotion; the new novel lies uncut; the magazines and newspapers fill their columns with extracts.' Sadly, he went on, at the same time 'histories of great empires, written by men of eminent ability, lie unread on the shelves of ostentatious libraries'. Macaulay argued that history, too, should have a vivid and dramatic character, and historians should not leave the exciting stories from the past to historical novelists like Walter Scott.[15]

Life-writing has become important for indigenous and minority historians, for it is in telling their own story that individuals from indigenous and minority groups can most easily communicate with people outside their group. There are many such works; perhaps the best-known Australian authors working in this genre are Sally Morgan, who wrote *My Place* (1989); Ruby Langford Ginibi, who has written a number of autobiographical books, including *Don't Take Your Love to Town* (1988); Leslie Marmon Silko's *Storyteller* (1981) and N. Scott Momaday's *The Naming of Rainy Mountain* (1969) blend a variety of oral and literary genres to deliver fresh perspectives on North American history.

Another form of history which focuses on the individual is microhistory. Important since the 1970s, microhistories tell a story about ordinary people in their local setting. Written in reaction to macro social science-style histories that generalise and seek the typical, microhistories narrow the focus and concentrate on the individual and the small community. They frequently look not for the typical but for the non-typical, the fortunes of the unusual individual being seen as affording a better perspective on social customs, mores, expectations and values. The not-so-ordinary individual has usually come to the notice of the authorities in some way, perhaps figuring in some kind of court case or inquiry. These sources afford a glimpse into the thinking of people who have otherwise left little or no written record.[16]

Historians of French and Italian history have developed the art of microhistory to a high level. In the 1970s and 1980s, texts like Emmanuel Le Roy Ladurie's *Montaillou* (1975), Carlo Ginzburg's *The Cheese and the Worms* (1976), and Natalie Zemon Davis' *The Return of Martin Guerre* (1983) demonstrated the possibilities.[17] *The Cheese and the Worms* elucidated a great deal about 16th century forms of reading and thinking through a detailed study of an Italian miller. Ginzburg's aim, as expressed in his preface, was, in part, to 'extend the historic concept of "individual" in the direction of the lower classes'.[18] All these works suggest, implicitly or explicitly, that you can learn a great deal about the world of people in the past from the detailed investigation of a particular case.

In all forms of life-writing, your work will stand or fall on the ways you represent your central character's ideas and motivation, emotions and aspirations. You may have letters, diaries and other forms of communication from your biographical subject that give some indication of how that person saw the world, but there is still the problem of interpretation. Though historians continually describe the thoughts and actions of historical individuals, we have few theoretical tools to help us understand how best to do so. Very often, without realising it, we simply follow the idea of character developed in the 19th century realist novel; that is, we try to create our historical actors as psychologically coherent individuals. Recognising this, in the past few decades, a number of historians have wondered whether psychoanalysis might be useful for understanding the complexities of the inner life of people in the past – Peter Gay in *Freud for Historians*, for example, suggesting that historians become more familiar with Freudian theory. Psychoanalytic approaches, however, have proven controversial, with those who oppose them regarding them as fundamentally ahistorical.[19] Whichever view you take, it's important to think carefully about your conception of character, personality and psyche.

We think there are some temptations to be resisted in biographical writing. One is the teleological narrative, the biography that is written as if the life is a unified journey towards some particular end; for example, the moment or period when the person was at their most famous. Life is far more messy and surprising and incoherent than that, and a good biography should be able to convey those surprises.

Another common pitfall is the temptation to assume or claim omniscient knowledge. Biographies take a long time to research and write, rarely less than five years – often ten or fifteen or even twenty. The biographer has lived with this person a long time, has read their correspondence extensively, and followed them down every burrow. They feel they know the person well. Yes – they probably know their subject better than any other living person does, but there is still the unknowability of someone else's life (and indeed your own). Thus you should always respect your subject's alterity, and not claim to know things about them that you don't.

Resist the temptation to take sides. Many biographers seem to fall in love with their subjects, although the many biographies of figures such as Stalin and Hitler provide salutary reminders that the opposite can also happen.[20]

As biographer, you are likely to develop obligations to the family and descendants of your subject in the process of research, which you must honour. On the whole, try to avoid developing obligations that restrict your scope. Make it clear you are interested in being balanced and fair, and that if you find some negative aspects, you may feel bound to discuss them, alongside the positive. Perhaps you can show a family member a copy of something else you have written in advance, so they can see the kind of work you do.

If you are writing the biography of a literary figure, beware of using their fiction as if it were autobiography. It may be, but then again, it may not. The author may well have based her evocation of a certain kind of childhood on her knowledge of someone else's life or something she has read, not on her own life at all. Treat fiction *as* fiction, as the creating of an imagined world.

Most biographies are about people who are famous for something – politics, the arts, sport, philosophy, the law, military action, whatever. Be sure you are well versed in, and take very seriously, the field of their endeavour. You don't have to be an expert exactly, but you do have to learn a lot about it if you are to evoke them in a way that makes sense. Biographies that don't care about the fields of action their subjects cared about are rarely a good read, and they are not good history either.

Dialogue and quoting from primary sources

Try to represent the point of view of your protagonists directly; as much as possible, make your actors speak. *Show*, as well as tell. We historians would dearly love to be able to write dialogue, since dialogue, as novelists and playwrights know, is important for dramatising the conflicts and relationships between characters, for giving a freshness and immediacy to the story. Because of its narrative power, most novels have dialogue of some kind. Without it, everything seems to be at one remove.

Yet how, technically, can this be done in histories? For a long time historians invented speeches to convey in an interesting and dramatic way the thoughts and ideas of their protagonists. They wrote monologues or dialogues, with speeches by others. Thucydides was a master of the invented speech, dramatising conflicts over military decisions and the like. By the middle of the 19th century, however, historians increasingly regarded invented speech as taboo, its use taken to signify that the writer had crossed the line from history to literature, from fact to fiction. This taboo continues today.

Sometimes it is possible to write historically faithful speech. We can inflect our sentences with short excerpts from a range of sources – letters, diaries, published writings, parliamentary debates, government archives. Using court transcripts, with their verbatim reports of accusers, accused, witnesses, advocates and judges, we can sometimes write dialogue. Or we may reproduce dialogue from the records of interviews conducted by commissions of inquiry, from the transcripts of parliamentary debates or, for more recent times, sound recordings and oral histories.[21]

In *The Slave Ship: A Human History*, Marcus Rediker uses dialogue from an inquiry to shocking effect. When Captain James D'Wolf suspected a female slave of having smallpox, he hoisted her on a chair and threw her overboard. A crew member by the name of Cranston is giving evidence to an inquiry:

> Q: Did you not hear her speak or make any Noises when she was thrown over – or see her struggle?
> A: No – a Mask was ty'd round her mouth & Eyes that she could not, & it was done to prevent her making any Noise that the other Slaves might not hear, least they should rise.
> Q: Do you recollect to hear the Capt. say any thing after the scene was ended?
> A: All he said was he was sorry he had lost so good a Chair.[22]

Used well, quotations give the text life, concreteness, immediacy, sharpness. Consider John Demos' story of the life of John Williams while the captive of Native American tribesmen. He is quoting from Williams' memoir of 1707:

> There are days out for hunting – on one particular Sabbath 'my master ... killed five moose' – and days also for roasting and drying the fresh meat. There are periodic encounters with other Indians, including, finally, 'my master's family'. The two men, 'master' and captive, share an increasingly complex – and close – relationship. At one point soon after the splitting of the main group, the master approaches Williams 'with my pistol in his hand'. He says: 'Now I will kill you, for ... at your house you would have killed me with it if you could.' But he does not pull the trigger. Later, he shows

'surprising' kindness and consideration: makes for his prisoner a pair of snowshoes, provides the 'best food' possible, supplies 'a piece of the Bible', and allows frequent opportunities for prayer and Scripture reading. Bit by bit, the gulf between them narrows.[23]

Here's another example. This little story, from a personal letter to a historian, helps us relate to those who lived through wartime London:

> Geordie, a young engineer at the time, remembers the aftermath of a V2 attack on New Cross as follows: 'Two doors from me the husband and wife were at their gate laughing, she had just put a plate of sausages, bacon and egg on the table when the rocket went off, the plate exited the window and landed instead on the garden hedge. True, honestly, and it was considered a great joke at the time.'[24]

The above examples work, but be wary of quoting too often, or in long slabs. Too many quotations can make a text very hard to read. Quotations which are too long – well, most people simply don't read them. We know *we* don't. Readers skip over the quote to the next piece of ordinary text, for they are in the zone you, the writer, have created, and they want to stay in that zone, stay connected, with you, and not meander off into someone else's way of thinking and talking. So as a general rule (and every rule can be broken sometimes) keep quotes short.

Oral history

If the period of history being evoked is recent enough, one way to bring direct speech into historical writing is the use of oral history interviews, though this will be the direct speech of recent memory rather than from the past the historian wishes to evoke. Writers of recent history know that quotations from oral histories give their narratives a freshness they might otherwise lack. In addition, for popular audiences the voice of the interviewee, even though it may be referring to events and situations many decades earlier, conveys a greater sense of authority than that of the historian. It is for this reason that popular histories in film, television, and radio seek oral history interviews and voiceovers, relegating the voice of the professional historian to the background, if it is heard at all.[25]

In terms of readability, oral histories really do help stories come alive. See how these excerpts from interviews with former soldiers in the Pacific campaign enliven Robert F. Jefferson's account of African American troops in the Second World War.

> As they proceeded through this seasoning process, newly arrived 93rd servicemen encountered unfamiliar sights, smells, and noises in the dense terrain. Edwin Lee, a 25th Infantry medical officer assigned to the Guadalcanal during the period, recalled, 'It was a disturbing experience for me to be on this island; nothing but trees, the smell of dead animals and sometimes human beings. I think the thing that stands out in my mind most is the rain every day at two o'clock and the lonely nights in which you could hear all sorts of sounds.'

Jefferson continues with more quotes that emphasise the dampness of the Solomon Islands:

> Private Bismark Williams, a native of Asheville, North Carolina, echoed these sentiments: 'The weather was damp and muggy, so it was necessary to keep your boots dry to avoid jungle rot.' Houston resident Asberry McGridd, an enlisted man who trained with a platoon in the 368th Infantry on the Russells, claimed, 'Unless you took care of your things properly, your clothes became rotted and mildewed and your weapon rusted.'[26]

(Note how we broke that quote into two parts. As one piece it would have been too long, and you probably wouldn't have read it.)

Oral history poses writing problems of its own. How faithful do we have to be to the interview transcript? What room is there for editing for the sake of clarity and communication? Can we edit quotations taken from an interview in such a way that we make what the person said to us more accessible to the reader, while respecting the integrity of the interview itself? Can and should we avoid 'cleaning up' a transcript so that it represents 'proper English'?

We think you should try as much as you can to retain the informant's distinctive style of speech, which might reflect their class or ethnic backgrounds. Idiosyncrasies and distinctive words and constructions add character, special nuances and meanings. You can, though, for the sake of readability eliminate the umms and errs and repeated words. People have spoken to you because they wanted their story told, so you can, with permission, do the editing and quoting that helps this happen. When you are checking transcripts and/or quotations with your interviewees, you can deal with any issues or problems then. Ann Curthoys has had the experience of showing the transcript to one of those she interviewed, an English teacher, who corrected her own words so heavily that they lost all the freshness and feeling of natural speech. This is unusual, however; most people are content to correct errors (the spelling of proper nouns and the like), if they correct anything at all.

Moral judgment

Should we express our moral judgments about the actions of people in the past? On this issue, historians are remarkably inconsistent. In E.P. Thompson's famous words, we should avoid 'the enormous condescension of posterity'.[27] We should immerse ourselves in the framework of thinking of the past, and develop a sense of why the people of the past acted as they did. We should have some humility, and be aware that future generations might think *our* values and actions highly questionable – as would past generations.

Yet historians don't really follow this idea through. We do see some actions as bad and others as good, even across the divide of time and circumstance. We do, that is, have a sense of common humanity that transcends time and space. Most of us would not wish to write about the Holocaust as if there were an open question as to its morality; most of us would find it hard to write about war without some sense of tragedy, and find war writing that lacks that sense very odd indeed. We do have strong feelings about what is good and what is bad, and to eliminate these entirely from our work would make it not only dull but perhaps a little distasteful as well.

So, what is the way through this dilemma? You might well have strong moral convictions, which will inevitably affect what you choose to research and write about, and equally inevitably will inform your work. Nevertheless, you should try to understand other people's motivation, ways of thinking, feelings and perspectives as well as you can. You should especially try not to use your knowledge of what happened next to pour scorn on those who did not know where their actions would lead. If you feel you must express your opinions of the people of the past, you should do so with care and restraint.

Don't hector the reader. If you do want to express some kind of moral judgment, try not to sound cocky, and do it taking into account the contemporary context of your study. In writing the introduction to *Contested Ground*, Ann McGrath had been worked up about the divisive, racist arguments in response to the then recent decision of the Australian High Court, the Mabo Judgment (1992), which officially recognised native title rights for the first time. She injected what she thought was passion into the prose in the first page of chapter 1. As it happened, and remember this was quite a while ago, her publishers asked Ann Curthoys to be a reader. Ann Curthoys responded by singling out the first paragraph of chapter 1 as 'hectoring'. 'Avoid hectoring,' she wrote. While Ann McGrath respected most of the advice, she got on her high horse and wouldn't change the paragraph. At the time, she had wanted to wear her anti-colonialism zealotry like a shiny badge. As it turned out, she now detests that paragraph and fears it may have stopped anti-land rights readers, the very people she was hoping to convert, from persevering with the book.

Ann Curthoys

I read Winthrop D. Jordan's famous and influential study, *White Over Black: American Attitudes Toward the Negro 1550–1812*, in 1969, while I was doing my PhD on race relations in colonial New South Wales. It was a new book then, and has since come to be regarded as an outstanding work in American history. It had a major influence on me, and reading it still moves and impresses me. It is both passionate and judgmental, as well as full of original research, and beautifully written. Listen to his prose:

Within every white American who stood confronted by the Negro, there had arisen a perpetual duel between his higher and lower natures. His cultural conscience – his Christianity, his humanitarianism, his ideology of liberty and equality – demanded that he regard and treat the Negro as his brother and his countryman, as his equal. At the same moment, however, many of his most profound urges, especially his yearning to maintain the identity of his folk, his passion for domination, his sheer avarice, and his sexual desire, impelled him toward conceiving and treating the Negro as inferior to himself, as an American leper.

Further down the page we come to his devastating final sentences:

If he [the white man in America] came to recognize what had happened and was still happening with himself and the Negro in America, if he faced the unpalatable realities of the tragedy unflinchingly, if he were willing to call the beast no more the Negro's than his own, then conceivably he might set foot on a better road. Common charity and his special faith demanded that he make the attempt. But there was little in his historical experience to indicate that he would succeed.[28]

Unless you are writing an expert witness submission for a legal hearing, you do not have to disguise your passion and enthusiasm. Passion can add energy, integrity and authenticity to your prose. Just because you are an author/historian, you don't have to feign being a non-person. Passion can be infectious, provided that it doesn't become preachy or polemical, and doesn't hector the reader. Good writing gives the reader a chance to understand your empathetic engagement with the past and the strength of your convictions.

10

Footnote fetishism

QUOTES AND NOTES

> *The footnote is not so uniform and reliable as some historians believe. Nor is it the pretentious, authoritarian device that other historians reject.*
> ANTHONY GRAFTON, *THE FOOTNOTE*[1]

While the last few chapters have been exploring history's literary affinities, this one inspects its more forensic side. We look at two key aspects of historical scholarship that most historians, especially beginners, find quite tricky. One is how (and how often) to refer to the work of other historians, and the other is the footnote (at the bottom of the page) or endnote (which is simply the footnote moved to a block of notes at the end of the chapter or the end of the book). Both aspects are hugely important for good professional historical writing.

Quoting other historians

Why *do* historians place so much emphasis on demonstrating their engagement with existing scholarship? First, there is the simple matter of good manners – to acknowledge the groundwork for your own endeavours and to show that you are working from solid building blocks. In the words of the American Historical Association: 'Practicing history with integrity means acknowledging one's debts to the work of other historians'. Do not build on just anyone's work. Rely upon and cite reliable authors of standing who publish in credible places and whose work has been peer or professionally reviewed. Acknowledging a debt to a lunatic fringe author who self-published (with the aid of an uncle's photocopying machine) may not be a good move.

Another reason to quote is to demonstrate how your own interpretation varies from preceding work. That is, you are helping your readers see what you are doing, where you fit in, and what they can gain from reading your work. You are demonstrating that history is not an open and shut case, but an ongoing project of research, interpretation and argument. The reader thus becomes part of a continuing historical conversation on your particular topic, for our discipline believes that all history is an unending conversation between the present and the past.

Locating a historical work in relation to others is very important when you are writing for professional books and journals, and even more so for a PhD thesis and in applications for research funding. But it is not always easy to decide how much referencing is necessary, or whether to do it in the text or a footnote. Too little referencing might suggest you are making it up, for you haven't demonstrated how you can truly *know* this information. Too little also fails to convey the importance of other people's work to your own work. Refer to others as necessary and always (in text or footnotes) when you owe a genuine debt for your ideas.

On the other hand, too much quoting and referencing of others sounds as if you don't have the courage of your convictions. You should avoid the common pitfalls of quoting endless authorities to say the simplest thing and qualifying every statement so heavily that it is easy to lose the main point. Also beware of being so even-handed and careful that you end up saying hardly anything. Don't be afraid to make your own argument. That is, after all, *why* people are reading your work.

Ann McGrath recalls her difficulties on this issue

So that my work 'looked' like a trade book, read like a lilting narrative, and featured only the people living in the time period it covered, I extracted references to the key recent theoreticians from the various chapters. But then I put them all back. In? Out? What was the right thing to do? To mention them in the text, or just refer to them in the footnotes? Was one strategy more honest than the other? Did I put them back just to seem more impressively academic?

You can refer to the work of others in a variety of ways. Some historians prefer the conventional literature review, where the relevant secondary sources are outlined, issues and gaps identified, and the author's questions, approach and research methods discussed. This is especially common as an early chapter in the PhD thesis, and in briefer form in specialist monographs and journal articles. Other authors prefer to spread the references to their sources throughout their work, referring to a particular author's publications only when it relates to the story they are telling or the argument they are advancing. While it does depend on the particular genre, for scholarly historical works we usually suggest a mixture of the two, with a brief early review establishing the key arguments of the literature and then more detailed discussion when it becomes relevant to your narrative and analysis.

Always introduce your authors. Just as it's important to introduce your historical characters, it's important to introduce your discussion and quotation of other historians properly. At least say who you are quoting. Many PhD writers don't, simply quoting someone in the text without saying who it is, and leaving this vital piece of information to the footnote. A proper introduction to the first quote from a particular historian is not only his or her name, but also something about the person you are quoting – even if it is just 'the philosopher X' or 'the American historian Y' or the 'poststructuralist literary critic Z'. The only exception would be in a work designed for specialists where you can assume that the reader knows the field. Even then, some introduction doesn't hurt.

Quotations can give a precise sense of what other historians have written, which is especially important if you disagree with them, or are relying on them strongly for an aspect of your argument. Here professional standards and ethical considerations come into play. It is important to quote fairly, to represent the writer's overall position, and not to quote out of context, distort or overstate their argument. Where you disagree, present that person's case at its best, not its worst. Keep quotes short and telling – as with quotes from primary sources, discussed in chapter 9. Long quotes break the flow of your argument and many readers simply skip over them.

In short, have strong views and support them with illustration, argument, information and some direct quotations. After describing, evoking and representing competing points of view, you must eventually give your own. If you want to reach an audience, you need to have the courage of your convictions. So say what you mean – it's what readers want to know.

> **Don'ts for quotes**
> - Don't quote too much.
> - Avoid long quotes – break them up to analyse them, idea by idea.
> - Try not to end a paragraph with a quotation from someone else. Keep the last word for yourself.
> - If not quoting, use your own words.
> - Make sure the quote marks or the quoting indentation, *and* the footnotes, are there.

Plagiarism

Plagiarism is pretending someone else's words are your own. Yes, there are degrees of plagiarism. There's accidental plagiarism, lazy plagiarism, cheating plagiarism, ignorant plagiarism and student alterationism. Best to avoid them all, okay? Let's get it clear: no pleading ignorance. Plagiarism is a piece of writing that has been copied from someone else and is presented as being your own work.

Now that last sentence was plagiarism. Because it wasn't ours. When we googled 'plagiarism definition' we found these words on wordnet.princeton.edu/perl/webwn. It would not have been plagiarism if we had written: Plagiarism is 'a piece of writing that has been copied from someone else and is presented as being your own work'.[2] You will see that the quotation marks clearly indicate that these are someone else's words. Also, the endnote acknowledges where we found the information.

What if we just changed it around a bit? 'Plagiarism is when you copy someone else's work and present it as your own.' In this case, you wouldn't need to quote it, because the exact words are not replicated. Should it be cited, however, because it is not your own idea? It depends on the context. In this case, we don't need to, because it is a widely known and accepted definition. It is not an original idea being borrowed from someone else. If we did not know whether this was commonly agreed on or not, that would be a good reason to footnote.

Plagiarism and cutting corners are more tempting these days, especially for time-pressed students. The internet offers sample essays, and sites galore from purported experts – plenty of know-it-alls and obsessive enthusiasts – and tonnes of reliable historical information on institutional and privately funded information sites. Excellent journals and libraries of books are also accessible in electronic copy. Some students cut and paste direct from such sources and attempt to pass off the work as their own. Others cut and paste, then use the 'altering words around' technique to disguise their borrowings. Some of them, in a bid to be 'a little bit honest', then cite the original source. These strategies will not lead to good historical writing, because you need to devise your own narrative flow.

Don't hitchhike on someone else's historical thinking journey. Create your own. It's much more enjoyable, and much more rewarding. Although most professors find spotting plagiarism fairly easy, in the past it was rather time consuming to prove, requiring follow-up library research. Today's powerful Internet search tools make it easy to identify the origins of exact word clusters. Anti-plagiarism software tools will bust even semi-disguised efforts – all in a few clicks. (On a similar note, be careful when you use notes and excerpts of work compiled for you by an assistant.)

Something else to watch out for is someone else's words getting stuck in your head without your realising it, and unwittingly regurgitating them in your work; it also happens (fortunately rarely) that pure coincidences will occur. However, if you are publishing in an academic journal or book and even such accidental plagiarism has crept in, it can be humiliating. In extreme cases, plagiarism has spelt career disaster, and even vice chancellors and university presidents have been sacked for it. Plagiarism is serious – a form of academic fraud – and just not worth it. It's dangerous – so please pay attention.

Ann McGrath: The late discovery

You are working on a great topic. You have done the research. You have come up with a brilliant hypothesis. You have written a great conference paper. You have nearly finished turning it into an article. You have only to do a little last-minute checking and bibliographical add-ins. You suddenly find someone has very recently written on exactly the same subject. OUCH!

Do you ignore it, hoping others will not notice? When this happened to me, I admit I was tempted. However, there will always be someone out there who *has* read it – its author, for one. You *have* to acknowledge the work, point out what it does that is the same as you are doing, and what it does that is different. In fact, you are obliged to ensure your work *is* different. That you had not come across the other work up to this point is irrelevant. It is part of your scholarly obligation to track down relevant work on a historical subject. There is a scholarly conversation going on which you are now joining. It is reader and writer etiquette. Even if you found it late, you know about it. Don't pretend otherwise.

Popular texts

So far, so good. The real trouble with quotes and references starts when we seek to address non-specialist audiences – the general, educated audience that may be interested in your work. These readers will often find reference to other historians boring, beside the point, and inward looking. It signifies a history written not for them but only for other historians; it sounds 'clubby' and point scoring.

Referring to others need not be a turn-off. In his wonderful prize-winning memoir, *Walking the Camino*, Tony Kevin tells us about the good books pertaining to the history of Spanish pilgrimages.[3] As his journey proceeds, he names and discusses the books that have given him insight into places and people. There is a disarming honesty in his easy style; the books and their authors are his intellectual companions, and the reader gains a sense of sharing both his physical and intellectual journeys.

Leaving out references and acknowledgments goes against the grain for many historians, and seems very ungenerous. The highest-selling history book in Australia in 2008 was David Hill's *1788: The Brutal Truth of the First Fleet.*[4] While the book has sold tens of thousands of copies, historians have been consistently critical. One of their main concerns has been the author's failure to notice or cite other relevant work: Cassandra Pybus for one was shocked that Hill had seemingly not read any of the many previous historians on his topic. Not only did he not cite or show evidence of reading the last thirty years of historical work, but: 'His threadbare acknowledgments would lead you to believe that he has come to this story unaided by anyone other than his editor and the staff of the Mitchell Library'.[5]

To fail to read those who have written about the same events reveals unforgivable ignorance. To read them but not cite them appropriately is mean-spirited and suggests an unwarranted claim to originality. It's not good, either, to briefly acknowledge recent work and then ignore its implications for your own argument. While the protocols for journalists are somewhat different, with much less opportunity to cite and acknowledge, for historians it is a matter of professional ethics.

Footnote fetishism?

While others might not understand our strange habits, the footnote is definitely the hallmark of professional history. Anthony Grafton entertainingly tells their history in *The Footnote: A Curious History*, using very extensive footnotes himself in the process.[6]

Given that we do not conduct scientific experiments on our subjects or verify our findings through repetition and replication, we can show our fidelity to our sources by carefully citing their details and location (in archives, libraries and elsewhere) so that other historians can check and verify and scrutinise them. The citation of sources is both an assertion of authenticity and a form of humility. It offers others the opportunity to check and perhaps to modify the historian's findings by a new reading of those same sources, or to revise the historian's conclusions by reference to new sources altogether. These protocols and conventions help us specify the exact relationship between the history we tell and the sources we use. Footnotes are an essential part of the conversation between historians, and a considerable part of our training goes into getting them right. They leave behind evidence of your evidence. Plus, your research becomes a useful path slashed through the historical jungle.

The American Historical Association Statement of Standards says:

Honoring the historical record also means **leaving a clear trail for subsequent historians to follow**. This is why scholarly apparatus in the form of bibliographies and annotations (and associated institutional repositories like libraries, archives, and museums) is so essential to the professional practice of history ... It enables other historians to retrace the steps in an argument to make sure those steps are justified by the sources ... Finally, the trail of evidence left by any single work of history becomes a key starting point for subsequent investigations of the same subject, and thus makes a critical contribution to our collective capacity to ask and answer new questions about the past.[7] [*emphasis in original*]

To footnote or not to footnote: scholarship in popular texts

When they wish to reach a wide audience, historians often find it difficult to know what to do about footnotes. It is here that we particularly find our professionalism and our desire to communicate with a broad audience in direct conflict. Historians are uneasily aware that the public often does not like footnotes very much. Even where popular history texts have endnotes, they are used rather sparsely. Footnotes and endnotes seem to intimidate and irritate a history-hungry public, who regard them as merely academic and unnecessary, stolid and off-putting, taking away the pleasure of reading. What is essential in one context (the academic book or journal article) poses serious problems of accessibility in another (the popular text).

So, what to do? If it is a trade book, it is still usually possible to acknowledge others, though probably more briefly than one would do in a specialist monograph or article. Some publishers, however, refuse to include either footnotes or endnotes. Page citations might be permitted for quotes only. The only place to acknowledge other authors might be in a bibliography.

As a result of these pressures, some historians, when writing for a broader public, feel it necessary to minimise or remove their footnotes, perhaps replacing them with a bibliographical essay at the end of the book. English historian Simon Schama did this in *Citizens: A Chronicle of the French Revolution* (1989). This led to an interesting exchange: American historian Gertrude Himmelfarb chided him for it in a review, arguing that a bibliographical essay couldn't provide the same kind of information as a footnote on the relationship between a source and a particular claim by the historian. Schama defended himself on the grounds that he intended the book for a popular audience.[8]

Historians may thus find their professionalism and their desire to communicate with a broad audience directly at odds.[9] In our view, the challenge in writing for wider audiences is not to abandon historical conventions, but rather to adapt them. Very often you can include footnotes, but they will be endnotes whose presence is indicated by superscripts in the text, and which will be fewer in number and shorter in length than you would have in a scholarly text.

Some writers dispense with superscripts altogether, constructing their endnotes so that the reader can relate relevant pages to the endnotes. Discursive endnotes of this kind read something like this:

> Page 45. For the reference to 'cowardly fools' see the *Manly Herald*, 5 June 1952. John Moore made his maiden speech in the NSW Legislative Assembly on 12 May 1955; see *Hansard*, vol. XXV, p. 235. The details about the public meeting of 28 September 1957 can be found in a report in the *Sydney Morning Herald* the next day, p. 4.
>
> Page 46. The detail about the domestic architecture of Manly in the 1950s is drawn from Joseph Wilson, *The Twentieth Century Australian House* (Sydney: Allen & Unwin, 2006), 44–6.

And so on.

Whichever method you use, you can reduce the number of footnotes by working information such as the date of a newspaper item into the text. Some journals publish in two versions, one hard copy with no footnotes, and the other online with footnotes. *Griffith Review*, an Australian journal of opinion and discussion, does this, and is going very well.

Ann Curthoys

One option is to put the notes on the web. With *Freedom Ride*, my publishers insisted, very late in the process, that it have only a bibliography and no endnotes. If the endnotes were left in, they said, booksellers would not stock it.[10] With considerable reluctance, I decided to place the very extensive notes on the web. There was an upside, though: as I prepared the notes for the web I found that I could include a lot more information than I could have included in the book.

What to put in footnotes

How do you decide what goes into your text and what to put in the footnotes? In general, you need to footnote primary sources, direct quotations, and other historians where you have relied on their work. Beyond that, you can use footnotes to provide details that will be useful to a specialist reader but of little interest to most readers. To help writers decide when to footnote, historian J.H. Hexter suggested a rule which he called the 'maximum impact' rule: 'Place in footnotes evidence and information that if inserted in the text diminishes the impact on the reader of what you, as a historian, aim to convey to him'.[11]

This is a good rule as far as it goes, but it is not always easy to decide what information diminishes impact, and what enhances it. Many historians, in any case, do not really obey it. Too often we come across academic texts cluttered with details that interrupt the flow of the argument, that are really far too specific and complicated. On the other hand, we sometimes find texts with such long and interesting footnotes that the reader who doesn't look at them misses half of what is going on; the reader who *does* look at them tends to lose touch with the text.

Systems of footnoting

There are many different systems for endnotes and footnotes, but historians tend to use the Chicago humanities system. The Harvard system of in-text, bracketed short referencing, with a complementary biography, does not suit history writing so well because of our extensive use of unpublished letters, archival documents, and multiple sources that would, if listed in-text, keep disrupting the flow of the narrative. Some publishers, however, require it, so you may need to master the style.

One much-used guide is *Cite it Right: The SourceAid Guide to Citation, Research, and Avoiding Plagiarism*, which follows several American writing style guides, including those of the Modern Language Association, the American Psychological Association and the Council of Science Editors, as well as *The Chicago Manual of Style*. It is intended for students and other writers of research papers, in an academic context.[12] The book *Modern Researcher* also has all the technical details one could ever want.[13] Australian writers may prefer the Australian book *Style Manual: For Authors, Editors and Printers*.[14]

You will need to follow your publisher's guidelines, in any case; this is non-negotiable. Archives often have their own guides as to how you should cite material found in them. Given the plethora of guides, and the specific requirements of particular publishers and collecting institutions, we will not rehearse here the details of how to cite secondary and primary sources. We note just a few of the trickier points.

TRICKY POINTS

- The 'citing and sighting rule'. When you come across a section of text cited by another historian but want to use the same quotation for your own purposes, be sure to consult the original for yourself. If you cannot (for example, is it in an archive or library far from where you live), then give the quotation as your historian gave it and say in a footnote 'as quoted by X'. In other words, don't imply you have seen a primary source when you haven't.
- Link references. Always ensure the reader can decide which footnote relates to which piece of text, and how. If you gather your citations at the end of a paragraph (which publishers often encourage, to reduce the peppering of text with superscript numbers), then ensure it is still possible to tell which footnote reference is attached to which piece of text, if necessary by repeating a little of the textual information.
- *Ibid.* When writing your drafts, avoid the use of *ibid* to refer to a second sequential reference to the one item. Using a computer, it is so easy to move sentences and paragraphs around that it is very easy to lose sight of what *ibid* refers to. Use short titles rather than *ibid* in your drafts (we think they are often better in the final product too, but that depends on your publisher).

If all this seems rather forbidding, it isn't really. As you nail those footnotes, and get them exactly right, it is curiously satisfying. You've finished off your work, tied up the loose endnotes, and you can enjoy these threads of connection with a worldwide community of historians.

11

Tough love

EDITING AND REVISING

I was working on the proof of one of my
poems all the morning, and took out a comma.
In the afternoon I put it back again.
OSCAR WILDE

Learning to be a good editor of your own work is the secret ingredient of good writing. Involving new writing, redrafting and rewriting, editing is one of the most important stages of writing. Editing is like writing in invisible ink. As the end product of good editing is nicely flowing prose, the reader never sees the labour that was involved. Ann McGrath was astonished when her PhD supervisor once told her that he tortuously reworked every word of his prose: his writing always seems so effortless – witty, original, readable and flowing, from beginning to end.

Editing should be done both on hard copy and on screen. In the days before computers, editing was literally a matter of cutting and pasting pages and paragraphs, rewriting and retyping – and you quickly reached a point where you decided it was probably okay. Today you can keep on editing till you are happy with the result. When you get to the editing stage, though, print your draft. Don't try to edit your draft entirely on screen; you will see all sorts of problems on paper that you miss on screen. Interestingly, though, once you have done your hard-copy edits and start entering them into your electronic document, you will see on screen more things to change. Make these improvements too, and when you get to the end of the article or chapter, print it out again. Read the revised version in hard copy. If there are still problems, go through the same procedure again. Keep doing this till you are satisfied (or you have reached the deadline).

Editing is no mundane chore; it offers vast scope for creating a meticulous and pleasing product. It can be the most enjoyable part of writing. Just as a film editor plays an important role in shaping the feel, the meaning and the story of a movie, so you are shaping your narrative and your argument. Sometimes the editing brings out what is innovative in your piece, and sometimes it leads to the 'ah-ha', the breakthrough idea.

Be tough on yourself. Perhaps it is acceptable to nurture yourself one day – smooth over your prose, give it a gentle massage. Savour what you've written. Enjoy it. Become your own number one fan. And well you might, for the next day you're in boot camp. Be a harsh, stern critic. You are aiming to write to the very best of your ability. Then push it further. You did 100 push-ups yesterday. Do 110 today.

Ask yourself, what would your scariest potential critic think of this piece? Or someone you know, your worst enemy? How would your favourite historian respond to it? Don't try to *be* another author – that will definitely not work. And don't be defensive. Use these imagined critics to help you challenge yourself, to help you improve your prose and create more confident writing.

There are many kinds of editing: big picture, detailed, conceptual, structural, stylistic, and fact-checking editing. Then there's copy-editing, footnote and endnote checking, and proof-reading. Some of this is plain hard work, some is challenging, but the result can be deeply rewarding.

Starting your edit

Think about what you first hoped to achieve through your writing, and how you now hope the editing will improve it. Edit in relation to where you wish to place your work. Ask yourself these questions (and tick them off as you deal with each one):

- ☐ Is the introduction clear? Does it really introduce what I've actually written, or have I promised material and arguments that haven't materialised?
- ☐ Is the language suitable for this venue and for this audience?
- ☐ When I read it out loud, is it easy to read?
- ☐ Is the length right?
- ☐ Is it tightly argued and clear? Is it convincing?
- ☐ Do I have enough evidence to support my argument?
- ☐ Have I included too many quotes and broken up the text? Or should I add a few more to help nail my argument?
- ☐ Do I have any long quotes? Can I trim them?
- ☐ Is the conclusion strong?
- ☐ Have I followed the right footnote and endnote style for the proposed publication venue?

If it's a narrative history, there are more questions:

- ☐ Have I presented my individual characters properly?
- ☐ Have I included emotion?
- ☐ Have I included the look, sound, smell and feel of

things? Have I given a sense of the details of the physical environment?

☐ Are my dates correct?

☐ Have I built up tension and suspense, or does it all sound too inevitable, too neat?

☐ Is anything sounding like a list (dates, people, etc.)? This doesn't work except in a 'how to' book like this one. Historical publications should be in prose.

Lists and dense factual material should go in separate tables. You might also use diagrams, maps, graphs and other coded presentations of data. When you do, check that you have referred to them in your prose, and integrate this information carefully into your argument.

Signposts

Your first page must lead the way; street signs and other means of orientation need to be displayed here (see chapter 6). But not too many signposts – they can become obstructions to the flow of thought and prose.

Your last pages should explain where you've been and what you have resolved or what you hope others will build on (see chapter 6).

Sub-headings can be useful to indicate a change of content and topic (see chapter 8).

Exercises for achieving clear thinking and writing

1   For PhD students and book authors having trouble with introductions and conclusions: print out just the introduction

and conclusion to each chapter, then read them in sequence. Suddenly it becomes clear what the introductions need to do, how each one must be different, and how they relate to the chapter conclusions. Even if you don't print them out separately, you can sit there with the whole printout and read just the introductions and conclusions to each chapter; you will probably see quite quickly what needs to be done.

2   Explain your project in three words. Yes, three only.

3   Explain your project in one sentence.

4   Do a diagram of your project. Use circles and arrows to work out how the five main ideas connect with each other, and with others.

5   Re-read your favourite work of literature, or your favourite historian. Is there anything there that you can learn from, that you can adapt for your own work?

6   Find a wonderful work of art. Stare at it, walk around it. Think about whether it can teach you something about your own composition.

Cutting for word length

Many publishers and many teachers are extremely strict about word length. They have good reason. The teacher wants you to express your ideas concisely, and to come to grips with the main issues. The journal editor must fit a certain number of articles into a given number of pages. The publisher has marketing and cost considerations, and knows the lengths of books in your field. Too long and they cost too much, and as a result probably won't sell.

If you've done a word count, and realise that what you have written is way too long, you will need to work out what to cut.

Estimate how many pages you must cut. Are there any obvious big chunks that are not working? Watch them go ... nobody will notice. Turn a whole section into a few nicely honed sentences. Condense four paragraphs into one. These are the fastest ways to cut big-time.

Another method is to carefully scour every sentence for unnecessary words. Be tough. You will find them. Cutting words out of sentences, and shortening sentences, and cutting down paragraphs, can be a strategy for tight, appealing writing. You enhance your logic, making your piece read more lucidly. Trim it, and the reading experience becomes more enjoyable.

Trash and treasure

Optimism aside, the hardest thing about editing is deleting. It is like the kind of tough love sometimes required in child raising, the saying 'no'. You cannot indulge yourself. This is the bit you don't like doing. It can hurt. You have a relationship with this prose.

Ask yourself: What is really necessary? What is indispensable? What does this add to my narrative, my argument? Is it central to my purpose, or am I going off on a confusing tangent?

This may sound straightforward enough, but let's look at the scenario. You have worked hard to build up your prose. You now have a whole chapter, or a whole article, but it's far too long. Or perhaps you have an article where the logical flow is not quite working. Or it's waffly, with too many side-roads. Without realising it, however, you've grown attached to your creation. Perhaps you are especially fond of certain solutions, certain paragraphs. They may be your favourite bits, composed of carefully polished sentences. But a piece of writing must work as a whole. You cannot retain even the most beautiful sentence if its presence confuses the reader about where you are going next. A confusing paragraph can blur the overall intent. Sometimes the smartly put words, the imaginative metaphor and the clever sentence do no service to the whole.

Let's face it; it is difficult to delete your favourite sentence. In this case, a bit of pop psychology might be helpful. The world can be divided into 'chuckers' and 'hoarders'. Some people are chuckers who love to clear their lives of junk. You lot don't have a problem; just use the trash can on your computer – or, if you still like writing in ink, a real litter bin. If you are a chucker, enjoy it. Delete wherever you can. Like a dieter watching kilos on the scales, savour the word count going down. This is an achievement to gloat over.

By their very nature, it's hardly surprising that numerous historians are hoarders. After all, they rely on archives and 'kept stuff'. Boxes of notes, correspondence, scribblings, old ephemera and mounds of books, accumulate into middens of deep time proportions. Only digitisation promises to save us from building extra rooms on houses or expensive storage fees.

How can a hoarder handle deletion? You make a special file. Rather than calling it 'Trash', 'Refuse' or 'The Unwanted', call it 'Treasures' or 'For Later'. Chances are you will never open that file again, but at least you know you've saved those beautiful words for posterity … they may come in handy one day.

Variety and liveliness

Check the flow and mix of sentences through your work as a whole. Simplicity is beauty. Lucidity is all. Intersperse short sentences with longer ones. Very short sentences can add drama and longer ones can introduce rhythm and flow. Just because your ideas are connected doesn't mean you have to fuse them into the one complicated, never-ending, multiple-clause sentence.

Is your prose zinging along? Or is it dead, dead, dead? If the latter, you obviously have a problem. For a heritage report or a piece of serious policy, it may be appropriate to adopt an earnest, serious, unembellished tone. But if your concern is to communicate to a wider readership, a general readership, and you want people to really enjoy reading what you have to say, make sure your work has plenty of interest value not only in its content, but also in its delivery.

You don't have to do anything fancy, but if your writing seems dull, ask yourself why. Think about how you can weave in something that will intrigue and fascinate, possibly even solve a mystery. Alternatively, hint at another spin-off story or meaning and leave your history reader wanting more.

Don't let your language get too flowery, or embellish it with too many adjectives. Unless you are writing a vampire history, avoid too much talk of the moon's reflection on the water, or of a girl's pale, delicate, dewy skin and fawn-like eyes. Clichés are dangerous. Two or three will be enough to give the reader the impression you are not an innovative writer, that you have nothing new to say.

Illustrations

At this stage, if you haven't already, you should be thinking about illustrations, maps, tables, and the like. All these can enhance your narration and argument enormously, but only if you think hard about what you really need and how to present them.

Find out what your publisher will allow in terms of number and type of illustrations. Sometimes you will be allowed none at all; other times, they will be welcomed or even expected. Illustrations may include drawings, sketches, engravings, paintings and photographs, all of which can add immediacy to your writing, for they confront the reader with evidence of sensate, living people in their own contexts. Their inclusion should never be gratuitous, however – they should be an integral part of the story or argument. A picture may be worth a thousand words, but that doesn't mean it speaks for itself. You as historian should comment on it in the text, and in a caption. A caption does not have to be one line only – it can offer insights into the photograph or painting, drawing attention to the subject's pose and clothing, the props, the painted backdrop, in the context of the technology and conventions of the day.

Make sure you have permission to use a visual image. Sometimes the use of a photograph can be quite traumatic for a family. Find out about any relevant cultural protocols: some indigenous peoples have taboos on photographs of deceased people, either in general or for a specified period of time, so make sure you have permission from the family or community to use the image. In the later 19th century, children were sometimes photographed after their death. To modern readers such images can be distasteful, as can photographs of skulls or other corpses.

Maps are important; too often they are missing from history books just when they are needed. If your book is the story of a journey, then at the very least you need a map showing the route taken. Sometimes your publisher will assist in the production of maps; other times, you have to organise this yourself.

Checking your spelling, punctuation and voice

We suggest you always set your computer to do a spelling check and a grammar check, and set the language tool to your particular brand of English – Australian, Canadian, United Kingdom, American, and so on, as the case may be. Checking programs can be excellent, but use them with caution for they are most likely to direct you to American forms of spelling, grammar and usage, whether you want them or not. They may also contradict the style guides provided by your publisher. That said, they do help you pick up many errors.

If your computer grammar check thinks a sentence is dodgy, it is well worth rethinking. Read carefully through it.

Such programs won't pick up all typographical errors. In fact, this kind of error can sometimes be autocorrected into a proper word – without your consent. It may not be the word you want, and it may not make sense, but it can be close enough for you to miss it. Your computer program will be so pleased with it, it won't even draw it to your attention. For example: 'can' in the second sentence of this paragraph lost its 'c' at one time and became 'an'; a 'this' could become a 'his'; a truncated 'plse' becomes 'pose'. In our draft of chapter 8, because the V was accidentally left off when 'The Vikings invaded Lindisfarne', the spell checker corrected it to 'The Icings invaded Lindisfarne'. Some autoformatting systems, thinking they are compiling a more orderly sequence, will change your dates a few decades or a few centuries, leading to embarrassing mistakes.

In chapter 8 we discussed when to use the active and passive voice. Even if you've done this already, now is the time to set your spell and grammar check to include style checking. It will alert you to every sentence using the passive voice. You will probably want to change the sentence to the active voice more often than not, but don't let the style checker be your boss. Keep the passive voice when it conveys the right meaning, puts the emphasis of the sentence where you want it to go and makes more sense, and sometimes keep it for variety, pace and rhythm.

While you are doing the spelling and grammar check, you are also doing a punctuation check. Or at least the computer program is. Colons and semi-colons can be tricky. You can be fairly sure the Word program assistant doesn't understand them either. Lynne Truss's very popular *Eats Shoots and Leaves* is an excellent guide to punctuation – she's both flexible and pedantic, in a nice way. Her title indicates the importance of punctuation.[1] So does this small anecdote, reproduced many times on the web:

> An English professor wrote the words 'A woman without her man is nothing' on the blackboard and invited his students to punctuate it correctly. His male students wrote: 'A woman, without her man, is nothing.' His female students wrote: 'A woman: without her, man is nothing.'

Colons usually denote lists: itemised things, concepts, people's names, organisations. That was such a list.

Semi-colons denote a clause with a verb closely linked with the previous clause. In her history of the American west, Patricia Limerick writes: 'Even in the earliest phases, mining required some expertise; rewards fell to those who knew enough to choose good claims and to develop them appropriately.'[2]

Full stops (periods) and commas can assist with simplicity and clarity. Think of them as providing a handy pause. Or as a dry spot to prevent one paint colour bleeding into another. Juxtaposed words can unintentionally distort the meaning, for in English the sense of the same word can differ according to placement and context. Stops and commas divide each point and delineate separate meanings. Commas separate clauses to indicate a conceptual break. In American English, commas are more popular between phrases and clauses than in British English. This also varies between individual authors.

If you are confused about where to put commas and full stops, try reading something aloud and noting where you would logically pause, and where pause is necessary and useful to the sense of what you want to say.

Capitalisation depends on context. Writing for public inquiries (or referring to them) generally requires upper case formality. In most publishing houses, however, there is a tendency towards lower case. The Northern Hemisphere is now often the northern hemisphere. These rules can be tricky, but it is best to follow publisher's guidelines unless you have an ideological objection or a particular point to make. For example, the word 'indigenous' spelt with lower case can refer to indigenous peoples generally; 'Indigenous' may reflect usage in a particular society. Australian authors now generally use upper case for the nation's Indigenous people, but this is not done everywhere. Explain to your publisher the political nuances of using the upper case in similar situations.

Make sure the indentations indicating new paragraphs are just where you want them. Where you have an indented quote followed by some of your own text that is meant to be part of the same paragraph, don't indent the line that comes immediately after the quote. Often this will happen because of the way you have set the tabs on your computer, so double check.

Fact checking

History must be accurate, so get it right. If you haven't checked back to a primary source during the course of several drafts, mistakes might have crept in, and it could be worth going back to key sources. Is the sequence of events correct? Do you have the right initials for people's names; are the locations spelt correctly and/or consistently; is the quoted prose word-for-word accurate?

Your computer spell check will not pick up date errors. You could mistype the numbers in the wrong order and get a century or two out of whack. Check this kind of thing carefully. Getting the decade or century wrong can make you look somewhat amateurish, as in: 'American Neil Armstrong's heavily-clad but virtually weightless feet touched down on the dusty moon on a cool day in 1869.' (By the way, was this day cool on earth or on the moon?)

Quote checking

If you are quoting another author, it is very easy to get a word or two wrong – especially if your handwriting is sloppy or if you are typing at speed without paying great heed to exactitude. In addition, the autocorrect functions on your Word program can be a nuisance: they fix up antiquated spellings and pester you about not using proper grammar when you are citing historical quotes, or partial sentences. So you might need to turn off the autocorrect button and when you're proof-reading a quotation on screen, make sure you cautiously scrutinise every suggested change.

Footnote checking

Given all we've said about footnotes, it follows that it is extremely important to get them right. Few historians would be so foolhardy as to claim they had never made a mistake in their footnotes, and we all hope that we have not slipped up somewhere, to be 'discovered' by a hostile critic. Ann Curthoys sometimes has nightmares that she has made a mistake in her footnotes and is being called up before an unnamed History Board in her pyjamas. (We warned you other people think historians are strange …)

We just hope such mistakes are as few and as inconsequential as we can possibly make them. So, some important advice: once you have finished your manuscript, *check your footnotes*. Because there have been major historical disputes based on mistakes in footnotes, it's worth being very careful. Where mistakes seem to be random, it is put down to sloppy scholarship, but where they tend to conform to a pattern, the matter becomes more serious. The errors may be a result of the historian's preconceptions influencing what he or she judges to be relevant or, more seriously and unusually, the result of a historian consciously misrepresenting the meaning of documents. (This is a difficult issue, for there will always be a range of legitimate disagreements over what a document means.)

How much checking? At the very least, check any footnote that you have any reason whatsoever to think needs checking. Some historians recommend checking all your footnotes at this stage; others check selectively. We generally check direct quotations and a certain portion of the footnotes, depending on the nature of the work. We don't check absolutely everything, but if we had a research assistant who was willing to do the hard yards, we probably would. While, ideally, you have been careful in taking note of, or copying, the original, you would be surprised how easy it is to make small mistakes: in spelling (especially of proper nouns), punctuation, and in the dates or page numbers in your footnotes. It is very hard not to make mistakes, with so much material to be organised, but it is important to CHECK, CHECK, CHECK to reduce them to the lowest possible number.

Permissions checking

Have you got permission to reproduce an image, an excerpt from a poem, an excerpt from an interview? Follow up and check all this in advance of submitting your work for publication. Be warned: getting permissions can be extremely time consuming. It is often difficult to find out just whose permission you need. You have to persist. Sometimes you will be asked to pay a fee.

Proof-reading

Proof-reading is for grammatical and expression glitches as well as for typographical errors. You should learn to be a good proof-reader of your own work. Read it right through. Then leave it a day. Read it again. Sliding a ruler under each line as you move down the page can help – it forces you to forget the forest and focus on the trees – and for proof-reading, that's what you need to do.

Then ask a fellow writer to read it. Or a friend or someone in your family. Fresh eyes are certainly needed, and they help when you really can't see the mistakes anymore. Sometimes you get that glazed-over feeling, where glassy eyes seem to match a tired, stilled brain. Only the next day do you realise you've used the same adjective five times in one paragraph, that the subjects within your sentences are lost, and that even *you* are unsure what you were trying to say. It may be embarrassing to expose your prose to the harsh light of day, but it is far more embarrassing to find a truly terrible mistake in the second line *after* you have already sent it away. Our advice: try not to press that 'Send' button until someone else has proof-read your work.

Acknowledgments

It's a nice gesture to acknowledge all the colleagues, peers, students, librarians, archivists, family members, friends, proof-readers and others who have assisted you. Keep a record of such people as you go – an acknowledgments file. Acknowledgments serve to demonstrate to your readers, especially your examiners, the personal effort, including the social effort, spent in research. Beware, though, of name-dropping, thanking people who are well known and whose assistance, if any, was minimal. One historian's acknowledgement of the Duke of Edinburgh in her book about women convicts is an example of taking the practice of acknowledgements a little too far.[3]

When your book is published, it's a nice idea to let those you have acknowledged know they have received an acknowledgment. Okay, we know we haven't always done that ourselves – we're sorry!

Going back to the source

If you are writing something, get it finished. Let too much time pass and it's so much harder to go back. Like an athlete, you might find the familiar muscular sequence is still there, but you need to gear up for weeks beforehand to get physically and mentally ready for the run.

Ann McGrath says:

Recently, I set out to rework a chapter that I first started on some years ago. My aim was to edit, cut and restructure it.

As I read, I began to wonder whether I agreed with my own arguments. I added many seemingly brilliant insights, most of which, on reading further, I found out I'd had before, for they came on later pages, often in better wording. Then I started to become bogged down. I began to think these scary negative thoughts: 'I am a really really bad writer ... I don't know what I want to say. It's all disorganised; it doesn't flow; it doesn't have anything new to say. It's not even interesting.'

The chapter was about Chinese, Pacific islanders and Aboriginal people on the Queensland frontier around 1900. Once it had been lively and fun, revealing exciting new sources to the world. Now it looked dreary, dreary, dreary.

What jolted me out of this morass was when I returned to my original notes, photocopies of letters and photographs from the Queensland State Archives and the State Library (John Oxley) of Queensland. The Chinese people in the photos were gathered at a police station, squatting on the ground, their queues or plaited pigtails wound around their heads in a decorative crown. Their clothing looked like standard issue from China. There was a loaf of bread and a billycan of tea in front of them, but they did not look happy. They were prisoners, perhaps indentured labourers on strike. A young-looking Aboriginal trooper stands in full uniform next to a white policeman. There is a sense of pride in his stance and on his face that suggest that perhaps it was he who found them. What a sense of power and control that would have brought to an Aboriginal person at this time.

There were other, later photos. One of a child about four, dressed in finely embroidered Chinese silks and a beautiful silk cap. Several old men with their teeth missing were happy to smile widely, standing proudly in front of dilapidated self-built slab huts. They looked so at home, so *with* their home. Some photos featured men carrying huge open woven baskets on a balancing pole, full of vegetables. And men with long boats full of bananas, whole bunches just picked from the trees.

My chapter changed. I was with people again, walking in company, so to speak, of people who lived. I felt excited. Now I could enjoy my chapter, for the voices caught in the letters and the fresh encounter with the photographs had woken up my socialising ability. Were these people still alive, I could hear them play music and entertain themselves and others. They had built their own houses out of local materials. I understood that agreeing to have these photos taken gave these men an opportunity to say that they belonged.

Going back to a primary source of any kind – archival letters, diaries, correspondence, paintings – can have the desired effect.

Responding to assessors' reports

Whether you are writing a specialist journal article, a short piece for a newspaper or magazine, a scholarly book, a trade book or a commissioned history, you will probably get assessors' or readers' reports of some kind. You need to respond carefully. On the one hand, you need to take the comments seriously, and if you are to be published, you should take appropriate action where you can. On the other hand, if the reports are so critical that they require you to completely change your argument or your approach, perhaps you need to try another publisher or another journal. You need to be flexible, and willing to learn from the comments of others, and yet retain your integrity as historian and writer.

Don't respond in the heat of anger or hurt. Nor if you're feeling tired, vulnerable, in an author-angsty mood. You might later regret a hasty vengeful reaction akin to road rage. Always give yourself a few days to consider a report, especially a negative one. Most assessors' reports will contain at least some criticism. Assessors feel that if they haven't made any suggestions for change, they haven't really done their job. A purely positive assessment sounds a little lazy (and perhaps sometimes it is). Some academic historians use assessments to show off their own wealth of knowledge, their sharp, wonderful minds. Ann Curthoys and co-author John Docker once withdrew an article from publication because the assessments seemed so negative and intrusive. They only learnt later that the comments were really quite mild for this journal, and they should have persisted.

Before submitting an article to a journal, assess whether it will fit that journal's thinking, style and subject matter. This can also be an issue with book publishers, especially with a themed series. Each case is different, but on the whole we think it's wise to respond to assessors' suggestions as much as you can. They very often help you strengthen your argument or your narrative. The assessors are not your enemy; they have been kind enough to read and engage with your work. Our three assessors for this book were tough and helpful, and we are truly grateful for their assistance.

Last words

Editing can be one of the most confronting, yet one of the most creative aspects of writing history. Leave yourself plenty of time for it. You'll need to do a complete draft before you really get stuck into full-on editing. But do not go on editing and editing into infinity. A good signal for when to stop is the moment you notice yourself changing back a word or a paragraph or, like Oscar Wilde in our epigraph, a comma that you'd changed only the day before. When you start to spend time worrying about whether the earlier version was better, STOP. It's time to let go, to move on to something else.

Epilogue

THE AFTER PARTY – MARKETING, CELEBRATING AND REVIEWS

Launching your book, radio program, documentary or film, website, or exhibition, celebrating its release, is not just about the party; it's about marketing, gaining attention, and starting it off on its long journey of academic and wider public engagements. The book is out, now you want people to read it. You want it to sell. You want people to enjoy it, and for your ideas to have an influence.

Your first task is to assist your publisher in marketing it so that your potential readers know it's out there. Help the publicist with the whole range of techniques used for its promotion, including lectures, literary lunches and author tours – bookshop signings, radio and press interviews, and talks to local history or community groups. Don't start promoting the book before it comes out – if people are interested, you want them to be able to find it in a bookstore.

Think about ways in which you can build your media profile. Offer an opinion piece to a newspaper. Relate your book to some current topic of public debate. Include the book's publishing details with your copy. Use your academic networks, and follow up any indications of interest personally. Be prepared to do radio and television interviews and if you're inexperienced, consider getting some media tips or training first. Double check that the producer knows the details of your book so that he or she can mention it on air. Learn how to have your key points prepared, and how not to sound defensive or hostile, even when you feel your work and, indeed, your reputation, are under attack. If you are pitchforked into an interview with somebody who disagrees with you, try not to sound shrill or confrontational. Instead, use it as an opportunity to let people know what *you* think and what your book actually says.

You could also set up a blog or website, with links to your publisher and to bookstores. Let your publisher know when you are speaking at conferences or other meetings, and take some book flyers with you. Always have flyers available when you give talks about the book, or are speaking on the subject you've written about.

Other post-publishing follow-up

- Ensure that your publisher sends the book out for review to all the relevant journals locally and internationally; prepare a full list yourself.
- Ask your publisher to nominate your book for prizes, especially if it has attracted good reviews.
- If your book is significant, see if colleagues will organise a panel to discuss it and related works – either a special event or a conference panel or afternoon symposium.
- Cultivate your networks so that you are invited to appear at writers' festivals and speak at other relevant events.

The book launch

Book launches can also help market your book, though they are generally less effective than the other techniques suggested above. Very often the people who attend already know about the book and plan to buy and read it anyway. For this reason, in North America and the UK, book launches are not necessarily held, and if they are they're no big deal. In Australia, what began as an event put on by publishers for booksellers has morphed into something mainly organised by the author, with some publisher's assistance. Although it will involve a few speeches, it's basically a party. It usually comes with some wine and food, and possibly music. Never organise a launch, though, until you're absolutely certain that sufficient copies of the book will be available.

A book launch really is a form of celebration for the author's friends, colleagues and family. It is like a life-cycle event; the book has taken some years to write, and its appearance in the world marks a kind of birthday. These days, we are so busy working that we rarely take a breath to enjoy and appreciate our own achievements, or those of our peers and colleagues. A launch enables the author to feel the book is really out there; it alerts the people closest to you that the book exists. It is an opportunity to thank those who've helped, to acknowledge publicly your appreciation of their contributions, even those who sent you to university or brought you up. One author invited an inspirational secondary school teacher to his book launch, which was a lovely touch and much appreciated by his former teacher.

A book launch can also sometimes be quite a serious event. Books can be launched at a conference, or an afternoon symposium held to discuss the book's contribution to its field, or a joint symposium with authors on a similar topic. The launch can become the occasion for the first serious discussion of the book, either in the launch speech or in a special panel discussion to mark the occasion. This happened when Ann Curthoys launched *Freedom Ride: A Freedomrider Remembers* in Sydney in 2002. Hundreds of people came – including former freedom riders, many Aboriginal people, especially from Walgett (a tiny town many hundreds of kilometres from Sydney and a focal point of the story), and many Sydneysiders interested in the struggle for Aboriginal rights. At the forum held after the speeches, many young people asked questions of the freedom riders present (such as 'Were you afraid?' and 'How can we do something now?'). Several Aboriginal people, who as teenagers had seen the Freedom Ride bus pass through their towns, gave emotional speeches about what they remembered of those times. It was a very moving occasion and many books were sold that night. The book was now truly out in the world – its meaning and value already tangible.

Sometimes a launch has a wider reach, especially if the book is about something of current political importance, or is launched by a celebrity or a politician. Journalists rarely consider book launches to be 'news', but the presence of a celebrity speaker or politician may entice them.

With less newsworthy books, use your own networks. The local market for *Civil Society, Religion and Global Governance: Paradigms of Power and Persuasion* (Routledge, 2007), edited by Helen James, was not necessarily obvious. Nevertheless, Helen put together a list of church leaders, human rights activists, politicians, lawyers and a range of people who really cared about its contents and wanted to read it. The crowd included at least one bishop and a vast array of influential people who would ensure that the book's ideas were taken on board beyond the academy.

Some official launchers will go on to write a significant review of your book in a newspaper or journal. A sitting High Court judge and well-known commentator on the legal system agreed to launch a book edited by Iain McCalman and Ann McGrath, on historians and the legal system and entitled *Proof and Truth: The Humanist as Expert*, at Law Society headquarters. It did not attract a huge crowd of fellow academics, but it attracted friends of the judge, among whom were the most senior legal counsel and most prominent legal thinkers in the city. The editors therefore achieved their goal – that lawyers would take the book seriously. High Court Judge Michael Kirby gave a brilliant critique of the book which he later published in a top legal journal, recommending the book as a text for law students. A good launch speech can often form the basis of a very useful, well-placed review.

After the party: dealing with criticism

We think it is important to learn from criticism, while not being intimidated by it. Beware of striking back with anger, or totally rejecting what your critics say.

When Ann McGrath saw the first reviews of her first book, she was stung to the core:

While lapping up all the nice things said, I only gloated for a short time, whereas the barbed comments kept me awake and made me angry. I knew some of the critics, and was stung that 'so-called friends' would publish such slurs on my book. I felt betrayed. The same people did not stop with one critique either. One gave a seminar on my book when I was sitting limply in the audience –

and where I was not given a turn to comment. Critics published book reviews, review articles, combined survey articles – and the list went on. I wrote one rejoinder in a journal, where I got on my high horse to restate what I was doing and defend myself against what I saw as vicious attacks. Some criticisms are irritatingly unfair; for example, one criticised me for not using a certain unpublished source whose authors had actually refused to release it to me.

Looking back now, I know this high level of attention was an excellent turn of events. The nature of academic scholarship anticipates a moving on, a development and progression. Authors can build on one another's contributions. It is if a great house is being built, brick by brick. These public, published criticisms meant many people were discussing my book, and the debate was recorded for future students to ponder and to make up their own minds.

In retrospect, we have often found the critics of our work have made quite a good point – a valuable point, even. The critiques of others are an engaged kind of discussion. Your voice is available in print; it is not the last word, and subsequently it is *other people*'s turn to talk. That's what ends up leading to historical debate. If your work becomes part of a debate, that's a good thing. You'll be noticed, you'll get citations; academics will place your work on course guides. Students love considering debates and learning how to conduct good historical critiques and arguments.

To sum up – yes, you may only want praise. It's human nature. But considered criticism reflects respect for, and engagement with, your work. It means it is being taken seriously. People are reading it. It's made an impact.

Equally, beware of believing everything the critics say. Some reviewers can be unfair or lazy or expect the impossible. Not all criticism is helpful, and the tone in which it's delivered is sometimes derogatory or insulting. Some people just can't behave well towards students or other colleagues. Perhaps your work challenges their preconceptions, or makes their own work seem moribund. Perhaps they are swiping back because you didn't pay enough attention to *their* work. Perhaps they are jealous or feel you've shown up their work's weaknesses. Whatever the reason, don't let them stop you. Nothing will be achieved if you are thin-skinned. Keep faith in yourself. Don't be intimidated or squashed into not writing.

Critics may bark, but even if they've gone further and actually bitten, it's still best not to take it too personally. Critics can be your new best friends. Reflect on your practice, use critique to empower yourself about rationale. Why did you do it this way and not their way? Harness the negative to turn it into a positive. Think of it as a painful workout. After the hurt, you'll improve. Talking about your reactions is important. And you do need to be receptive and open to criticism.

Enjoy any praise you may receive, but don't let it go to your head. Be tough on yourself and keep aiming higher.

Like some great ocean journey, writing your book or article has been full of both dangerous and pleasurable encounters. Mostly you have stayed afloat, but immersion also brought some adventures and new visions. Now, with its weighty souvenir, your journey has become tangible. Celebrate.

A cruise launch or a rocket blast? You decide. Do this before ... before ... what? Before getting back to your next project, of course. By the time your finished history appears, your next project has well and truly started. This guidebook, plus your now well-developed support network, can help you navigate another historical voyage in time for the next celebration.

Notes

Introduction

1   David Thelen, 'The movie maker as historian: Conversations with Ken Burns,' *The Journal of American History* 81, no. 3 (1994): 1031–50, 32.

2   Lucian of Samosata, *The Way to Write History*, c. 165 CE, in *The Works of Lucian, Vol. II*, consulted at <http://www.sacred-texts.com/cla/luc/wl2/wl210.htm>. The advice listed here is found in the paragraphs numbered: 27, 41, 43, 44, 45, 51, 56, 57, 59, 61.

3   Extract from Thomas Babington Macaulay's essay 'On History' (a review of Henry Neele, *The Romance of History. England*), first published in the *Edinburgh Review*, May 1828, 361.

4   G.M. Trevelyan, 'Clio, a muse', first published in December 1903 in the *Independent Review*. Reprinted in Fritz Stern, ed., *The Varieties of History: From Voltaire to the present* (Cleveland: Meridian, 1966), 227–45.

5   Herbert Butterfield, *The Whig Interpretation of History* (London: G. Bell & Sons, 1931), 105.

6   See also Hugh Trevor-Roper, 'History: Professional and lay,' in John Tosh, ed., *Historians on History: Readings* (Harlow, England: Pearson Longman, 2009).

7   W.B. Gallie, *Philosophy and the Historical Understanding* (New York: Schocken Books, 1964); Morton White, *Foundations of Historical Knowledge* (New York: Harper & Row, 1965); Maurice Mandelbaum, 'A note on history as narrative,' *History and Theory* 6, no. 3 (1967): 413–9; William H. Dray, Richard G. Ely & Rolf Gruner, 'Mandelbaum on history as narrative: A discussion,' *History and Theory* 8 (1969): 275–94.

8 J.H. Hexter, 'The rhetoric of history,' *History and Theory* 6, no. 1 (1967): 3–13. A longer version appeared in J.H. Hexter, *Doing History* (London: George Allen & Unwin, 1971).

9 Hexter, *Doing History*, 47–8.

10 Arthur Marwick, *The Nature of History* (London: Macmillan, 1970).

11 Hayden White, *Tropics of Discourse: Essays in cultural criticism* (Baltimore: Johns Hopkins University Press, 1978), especially chapter 3.

12 For example: Hazel Edwards, *Writing a Non-Boring Family History* (Sydney: Hale & Iremonger, 2003); John Charles Cox, *How to Write the History of a Parish* (BiblioBazaar, LLC, 2008); Anne D'Alleva, *How to Write Art History* (London: Laurence King Publishing, 2006); Martin M.G. Fase, Gerald D. Feldman & Manfred Pohl, eds, *How to Write the History of a Bank* (London: Scholar Press, 1996); Bob Trubshaw, *How to Write and Publish Local History* (Market Harborough, UK: Heart of Albion Press, 1999); Frederick E. Maser, *How to Write a Local Church History* (Madison, NJ: United Methodist Church, General Commission on Archives and History, 1990).

1: Which history to tell?

1 Marc Bloch, *The Historian's Craft* (Manchester: Manchester University Press, 1992 [first published 1954]), 22. NB: The 'good historian', including the giant, can also be a she.

2 Greg Dening, 'Reading to write', in Marion Halligan, ed., *Storykeepers* (Sydney: Duffy & Snellgrove, 2001), 33.

3 Benedetto Croce, *History: Its theory and practice*, trans. Douglas Ainslie (New York: Harcourt, Brace & Co., 1921), 11–26, reprinted as 'History and chronicle', in Hans Meyerhoff, ed., *The Philosophy of History in our Time* (New York: Doubleday Anchor, 1959), 45.

4 Joanna Bourke, *Fear: A cultural history* (London: Virago, 2005); Francesca Orsini, ed., *Love in South Asia: A cultural history* (Cambridge: Cambridge University Press, 2006); Jacques Gelis, *History of Childbirth: Fertility, pregnancy and birth in early modern Europe* (Cambridge: Polity Press, 1991); Rebecca Jennings, *A Lesbian History of Britain: Love and sex between women since 1500* (Oxford: Greenwood World, 2007).

5 Jackie Huggins & Kay Saunders, 'Defying the ethnographic ventriloquists: Race, gender and the legacies of colonialism,' *Lilith*, no. 8 (1993): 60–70.

6 Nancy Shoemaker, ed., *Clearing a Path: Theoretical approaches to the past in Native American studies* (New York: Routledge, 2002); Nancy Shoemaker, ed.,

Negotiators of Change: Historical perspectives on Native American women (New York: Routledge, 1995); Peter Nabokov, *A Forest of Time: American Indian ways of history* (Cambridge: Cambridge University Press, 2002).

2: Who is your history for?

1   Johann Huizinga, *Men and Ideas* (London: Eyre & Spottiswoode, 1960), 39.

2   See, e.g. William Kelleher Storey, *Writing History: A guide for students*, 3rd edn (New York: Oxford University Press, 2009); I.W. Mabbett, *Writing History Essays: A student's guide* (Houndsmills: Palgrave Macmillan, 2007); Jules R. Benjamin, *A Student's Guide to History*, 10th edn (Boston: Bedford/St Martins, 2007). Many history departments now provide their own online guides.

3   Ann McGrath, *Born in the Cattle* (Sydney: Allen & Unwin, 1987); American Academy of Learned Societies e-book, 2006. <http://www.humanitiesebook. org/acls.html>

4   Joan Wallach Scott, 'Introduction, A.H.R. Forum: Revisiting "Gender: A useful category of historical analysis",' *The American Historical Review* 113, no. 5 (2008): 1344.

5   Patrick Wolfe, 'Land, labor, and difference: Elementary structures of race,' *The American Historical Review* 106, no. 3 (2001): 866–905; Dipesh Chakrabarty, 'Postcoloniality and the artifice of history: Who speaks for "Indian" pasts?,' *Representations* 37 (Winter 1992): 1–26.

6   William Germano, *Getting It Published: A guide for scholars and anyone else serious about serious books* (Chicago: University of Chicago Press, 2001).

7   Eleanor Harman & Ian Montagnes, *The Thesis and the Book*, 2nd edn (Toronto: University Of Toronto Press, 2003).

8   Japan has a particularly centralised system for authorising textbooks. See Tessa Morris-Suzuki, *The Past Within Us: Media, memory, history* (London: Verso, 2005).

9   James R. Millar, ed., *Encyclopedia of Russian History* (New York: Macmillan Reference, 2004), vii.

10 Martin Marix Evans, *Encyclopedia of the Boer War: 1899–1902* (Santa Barbara, California: ABC-Clio, 2000).

11 Germano, *Getting It Published*, 6.

12 See Ann Curthoys, Ann Genovese & Alexander Reilly, *Rights and Redemption: History, law, and Indigenous people* (Sydney: UNSW Press, 2008); Iain McCalman & Ann McGrath, eds, *Proof and Truth: The humanist as expert* (Canberra: The Australian Academy of the Humanities, 2003).

13 For an example of a commissioned history which was rejected see Rachel Wells, 'A century of history for sale in biography of an emporium', *The Age*, 14 September 2008: <www.theage.com.au/national/a-century-of-history-for-sale-in-biography-of-an-emporium-20080913-4fyc.html>

14 Langston Hughes, *Fight for Freedom: The story of the NAACP* (New York: W.W. Norton, 1962), 203.

15 Jonathan Steinberg, in co-operation with the members of the Historical Commission appointed to examine the history of the Deutsche Bank in the period of National Socialism, *The Deutsche Bank and Its Gold Transactions During the Second World War* (Munich: Verlag C.H. Beck, 1999), 12.

16 Robert Fitzgerald, *Rowntree and the Marketing Revolution, 1862–1969* (Cambridge: Cambridge University Press, 1995); John F. Wilson, 'Review of Robert Fitzgerald, *Rowntree and the Marketing Revolution, 1862–1969*', *EH Net Economic History Services* (1995), <http://eh.net/bookreviews/library/0010>.

17 Richard White, *Remembering Ahanagran: A history of stories* (New York: Hill & Wang, 1998); Michael King, *Being Pakeha Now: Reflections and recollections of a white native* (Auckland: Penguin Books (NZ), 1999); Timothy Kenslea, *The Sedgwicks in Love: Courtship, engagement, and marriage in the early Republic* (Boston: Northeastern University Press, 2006); Annette Gordon-Reed, *The Hemingses of Monticello: An American family* (New York: W.W. Norton, 2008).

18 Ann McGrath, 'Must film be fiction?,' *Griffith Review*, no. 24 (2009).

19 Frank L. Cioffi, *The Imaginative Argument: A practical manifesto for writers* (Princeton, NJ: Princeton University Press, 2005), 22.

3: Crying in the archives

1 Tom Griffiths, *Slicing the Silence: Voyaging to Antarctica* (Sydney: UNSW Press, 2007; Boston: Harvard University Press, 2007), 21.

2 Tom Griffiths, 'The poetics and practicalities of writing', in Ann Curthoys & Ann McGrath, eds, *Writing Histories: Imagination and narration* (Melbourne: School of Historical Studies, Monash University, 1999), 3–4, also available from Monash University E Press, 2009, at <http://publications.epress.monash.edu/loi/wh>

3 Alan Ward, 'History and historians before the Waitangi Tribunal: Some reflections on the Ngai Tahu claim', *New Zealand Journal of History* 42, no. 2 (1990): 150–67. These words are Ward's own, from pp. 152–3, with some omissions and reformatting.

4 Henry Reynolds, *The Other Side of the Frontier: Aboriginal resistance to the European invasion of Australia* (Sydney: UNSW Press, 2006).

4: History in 3D

1 Helen Garner, *True Stories* (Melbourne: Text Publishing, 1996), 52.

2 Edward B. Tylor, *Anthropology* (London: Macmillan, 1881), 179.

3 Julie Cruikshank, 'Oral history, narrative strategies and Native American historiography: Perspectives from the Yukon Territory, Canada', in Nancy Shoemaker, ed., *Clearing a Path: Theorizing the past in Native American studies* (New York: Routledge, 2002).

4 Fernand Braudel, 'History and the social sciences,' in *On History* (Chicago: University of Chicago Press, 1980); Fernand Braudel, *The Mediterranean and the Mediterranean World in the Age of Philip II, Vol. 1* (London: William Collins & Sons, 1972); Ann Curthoys & John Docker, *Is History Fiction?* (Sydney: UNSW Press, 2006), 126–8.

5 John Berger, *And Our Faces, My Heart, Brief as Photos* (New York: Pantheon Books, 1984); John Berger, 'The ambiguity of the photograph,' in Kelly Michelle Askew & Richard R. Wilk, eds, *The Anthropology of Media: A reader* (Malden, MA: Blackwell Publishers, 2002); Jane Lydon, *Eye Contact: Photographing Indigenous Australians* (Durham: Duke University Press, 2005); Graham Clarke, *The Photograph* (Oxford: Oxford University Press, 1997); David E. Kyvig & Myron A. Marty, *Nearby History: Exploring the past around you*, 2nd edn (Lanham, MD: Roman & Littlefield, 2000), chapter 7 'Visual documents'.

6 Humphrey McQueen, *Suspect History* (Adelaide: Wakefield Press, 1997), 158–9.

7 See Graeme Davison, *The Use and Abuse of History* (Sydney: Allen & Unwin, 2000).

8 Ann McGrath, A. 'Being Annie Oakley: Modern girls, new world women', *Frontiers: A Journal of Women's Studies* 28.1, 28.2 (2007): 203–31.

9 Tim Bonyhady & Tom Griffiths, eds, *Words for Country : Landscape and language in Australia* (Sydney: UNSW Press, 2002), 1.

10 Manning Clark, 'A discovery of Australia,' in *Occasional Writings and Speeches* (Sydney: Fontana/Collins, 1980), 68; A.L. Rowse, *The Use of History* (London: Hodder & Stoughton, for the English Universities Press, 1946), 42–3. The origin of the quote is somewhat mysterious.

11 For a discussion of this kind of journalism, see Judith Walkowitz, *City of Dreadful Delight: Narratives of sexual danger in late-Victorian London* (London: Virago, 1992).

12 Matt Buchanan, 'Evolution of the modest hero: Iain McCalman talks to Matt Buchanan', *The Sydney Morning Herald (Spectrum)*, 14 February 2009, 26.

13 Luisa Passerini, 'Work, ideology and consensus under Italian Fascism,' *History Workshop Journal* 8, no. 1 (1979): 82–108. Reprinted in Robert Perks & Alistair Thomson, eds, *The Oral History Reader* (London: Routledge, 1998), 53–62.

14 Alessandro Portelli, *The Death of Luigi Trastulli, and Other Stories: Form and meaning in oral history* (Albany: State University of New York Press, 1991). See also Alessandro Portelli, 'What makes oral history different', in Perks & Thomson, *The Oral History Reader*, 63–74.

15 See especially Perks & Thomson, eds, *The Oral History Reader*.

16 Lorina Barker, '"Hangin' out" and "yarnin'"', *History Australia* 5, no. 1 (April 2008): 9.1–9.9.

17 Recording technologies change quickly, so earlier forms rapidly become outdated. A public institution will be better able to preserve, and provide the technology for reading, your taped interviews.

5: How to avoid writer's block

1 Amitav Ghosh, *The Hungry Tide* (London: Harper Collins, 2004), 148.

2 Robert Neale, *The Common Writer: Theory and practice for writers and teachers* (Auckland: Oxford University Press, 1991), 83.

3 Jack Kerouac, *Atop an Underwood: Early stories and other writings*, edited by Paul Marion (New York: Viking Press, 1999).

4 Mark Tredinnick, *The Little Red Writing Book* (Sydney: UNSW Press, 2006).

5 Neale, *The Common Writer*, 82.

6: Once upon a time

1 Lewis Carroll, *Alice's Adventures in Wonderland*, 1865.

2 Catherine Hall, *Civilising Subjects: Metropole and colony in the English imagination 1830–1867* (London: Polity Press, 2002), 1, 7.

3 Muriel E. Chamberlain, *The Longman Companion to European Decolonisation in the Twentieth Century* (London: Longman, 1998), viii.

4 John Hobson, *The Eastern Origins of Western Civilisation* (Cambridge: Cambridge University Press, 2004), x.

5 In a very helpful essay, William Dowling says the introductory chapter should 'stand almost as an essay in itself, except that it would be full of points that

begged for further elaboration': William C. Dowling, 'Avoiding the warmed-over dissertation', in Eleanor Harman & Ian Montagnes, eds, *The Thesis and the Book* (Toronto: University of Toronto Press, 2003), 50.

6 Mark Atwood Lawrence, *Assuming the Burden: Europe and the American commitment to war in Vietnam* (Berkeley: University of California Press, 2005), 4–6.

7 Anne Salmond, *Two Worlds: First meetings between Maori and Europeans, 1642–1772* (Auckland: Viking, 1991), 13.

8 Richard White, *The Middle Ground: Indians, empires, and republics in the Great Lakes region, 1650–1815* (New York: Cambridge University Press, 1991), 1.

9 Iain McCalman, *The Seven Ordeals of Count Cagliostro: The greatest enchanter of the eighteenth century* (Sydney: Flamingo–Harper Collins, 2003), 3.

10 Alan Atkinson, *Camden: Farm and village life in early New South Wales* (Melbourne: Oxford University Press, 1988), 1.

11 Carlo Ginzburg, *The Cheese and the Worms: The cosmos of a sixteenth century miller* (London: Penguin, 1992 [1976]), 1.

12 Lionel Gossman, 'Anecdote and history', *History and Theory*, 42.2 (2003): 143–68.

13 See William E. Engel, 'Aphorism, anecdote and anamnesis in Montaigne and Bacon', *Montaigne Studies: An Interdisciplinary Forum* 1, no. 1 (1989): 158–79; entry on 'Montaigne' in Britannica.com.

14 Lyndal Roper, *Witch Craze: Terror and fantasy in Baroque Germany* (New Haven: Yale University Press, 2004), 1, 4.

15 Mary Dudziak, *Cold War, Civil Rights: Race and the image of American democracy* (Princeton: Princeton University Press, 2000), 115.

16 Penelope Lively, *Moon Tiger* (London: Penguin, 1988), 1, 2.

17 Emmanuel Le Roy Ladurie, *Carnival in Romans: A people's uprising at Romans 1579–1580* (Harmondsworth: Penguin, 1981), 338–9.

18 See Peter Burke, ed., *New Perspectives on Historical Writing* (Cambridge: Polity Press, 1991), 239–40; Hayden White, *Tropics of Discourse: Essays in cultural criticism* (Baltimore: Johns Hopkins University Press, 1978), especially chapter 3.

19 Howard G. Brown, *Ending the French Revolution: Violence, justice, and repression from the Terror to Napoleon* (Charlottesville: University of Virginia Press, 2006), 2, 3.

20 Jane Lydon, *Eye Contact: Photographing Indigenous Australians* (Durham: Duke University Press, 2005).

21 Marcus Rediker, *The Slave Ship: A human history* (New York: Viking, 2007), 4, 355.

22 Les Carlyon, *The Great War* (Sydney: Pan Macmillan, 2006), 3, 777.

7: Narrative, plot, action!

1 Peter Gay, *Style in History* (New York: Basic Books, 1974), 189.

2 E.P. Thompson, *The Making of the English Working Class* (Harmondsworth: Penguin, 1968 [1963]).

3 Eric Hobsbawm, *The Age of Capital 1848–1875* (London: Abacus, 1997).

4 Linda Colley, *Britons: Forging the Nation 1707–1837* (London: Vintage, 1996), 112–22.

5 For a discussion of action-oriented history, see June Phillip, 'Traditional historical narrative and action-oriented (or ethnographic) history', *Historical Studies*, vol. 20 (1982): 339–52. For the idea of history as drama, see Greg Dening, *Performances* (Melbourne: Melbourne University Press, 1996) and Rhys Isaac, *The Transformation of Virginia, 1740–1790* (Chapel Hill: University of North Carolina Press, 1999).

6 Barbara Tuchman, *Practicing History: Selected essays* (New York, Knopf, 1981), 22.

7 Geoffrey Blainey, *The Tyranny of Distance* (Melbourne: Sun Books, 1966), 45–7.

8 Ann Curthoys, *Freedom Ride: A freedomrider remembers* (Sydney: Allen & Unwin, 2002).

9 Dominick LaCapra, 'Rhetoric and history', in *History and Criticism* (Ithaca, NY: Cornell University Press, 1985), 18–19, 38, 42.

10 Manning Clark, 'A discovery of Australia', in *Occasional Writings and Speeches* (Sydney: Fontana/Collins, 1980), 76.

11 Bill Gammage, 'The broken years: Australian soldiers in the Great War, 1914–18', in Ann Curthoys & Ann McGrath, eds, *Writing Histories: Imagination and narration* (Melbourne: School of Historical Studies, Monash University, 1999), 17; also available from Monash University E Press, 2009, at <http://publications. epress.monash.edu/>

12 Roland Barthes, *Mythologies* (London: Granada, 1979 [1957]).

13 Roland Barthes, 'Historical discourse', in Michael Lane, ed., *Introduction to Structuralism* (New York: Basic Books, 1970), 145–55, quote on 149.

14 Michel Foucault, 'Nietzsche, genealogy, history', in Donald F. Bouchard, ed., *Language, Counter-Memory, Practice: Selected essays and interviews* (Ithaca, NY: Cornell University Press, 1986), 71–2.

15 Wallace Martin, *Recent Theories of Narrative* (Ithaca: Cornell University Press, 1986), 130–51.

16 Inga Clendinnen, 'Fellow sufferers: History and imagination', *Australian Humanities Review* 3 (September-November 1996).

17 John Demos, *The Unredeemed Captive: A family story from early America* (New York: Knopf, 1994).

18 Martha Hodes, *The Sea Captain's Wife: A true story of love, race, and war in the nineteenth century* (New York: W.W. Norton, 2006), available at <http://seacaptainswife.com/>

19 Peter Burke, ed., *New Perspectives on Historical Writing* (Cambridge: Polity Press, 1991), 233–48, quote on 239.

20 Mikhail Bakhtin, *Problems of Dostoevsky's Poetics* (Manchester: Manchester University Press, 1984), 71.

21 Richard Price, *Alabi's World* (Baltimore: Johns Hopkins University Press, 1990).

22 Donald J. Raleigh, *Russia's Sputnik Generation: Soviet baby boomers talk about their lives* (Bloomington: Indiana University Press, 2006); Megan Hutching, *Last Line of Defence: New Zealanders remember the war at home* (Auckland: HarperCollins in association with Ministry for Culture and Heritage, 2007); Gerald M. Oppenheimer, *Shattered Dreams? An oral history of the South African epidemic* (Oxford: Oxford University Press, 2007).

23 Patsy Cravens, *Leavin' a Testimony: Portraits from rural Texas* (Austin: University of Texas Press, 2006), 80.

8: Styling pasts for presents

1 George Orwell, *Politics and the English Language*, 1946, available at <http://www.george-orwell.org/Politics_and_the_English_Language/0.html>

2 It began as a textbook by William Strunk, privately printed, for his English classes at the end of the First World War. In 1957, after Strunk's death, Macmillan commissioned E.G. White to revise the book for the college market and general readers. The Strunk & White version was so popular it was revised again in 1972, and 1979. White died in 1985, and a fourth edition, modified by an anonymous editor, appeared in 1999, with many subsequent reprintings.

3 William Knowlton Zinsser, *On Writing Well: The Classic Guide to Writing Nonfiction* (New York: St Martins, 2006 [1976]); Pam Peters, *The Cambridge Guide to Australian English Usage*, 2nd edn (Melbourne: Cambridge University Press, 2007).

4 Greg Dening, *Performances* (Melbourne: Melbourne University Press, 1996).

5 Greg Dening, 'Writing: Praxis and performance', in Ann Curthoys & Ann McGrath, eds, *Writing Histories: Imagination and narration* (Melbourne: School of Historical Studies, Monash University, 1999), 48; also available from Monash University E Press, 2009, at <http://publications.epress.monash.edu/loi/wh>

6   Mark Tredinnick, *The Little Green Grammar Book* (Sydney: UNSW Press, 2008).

7   Patricia Nelson Limerick, 'Dancing with professors', *New York Times Book Review* (31 October 1993), 23–4.

8   Thomas Babington Macaulay, *The History of England* (Harmondsworth: Penguin Classics [1849] 1979), 243.

9   Don Watson, *Watson's Dictionary of Weasel Words, Contemporary Clichés, Cant and Management Jargon* (Sydney: Vintage, 2005).

10   Robin W. Winks, *The Blacks in Canada: A history* (Montreal: McGill Queen's University Press, 1997), xv–xvi.

11   E.P. Thompson, *The Making of the English Working Class* (Harmondsworth: Penguin, 1968 [1963]), 410.

12   See Ann Curthoys & John Docker, *Is History Fiction?* (Sydney: UNSW Press, 2005), 152–3.

13   E.P. Thompson, *Poverty of Theory and Other Essays* (New York: Monthly Review Press, 1978).

14   Anthony Easthope, 'Romancing the Stone: History-writing and rhetoric', *Social History* 18, no. 2 (1993): 235–49, 46.

15   Nancy F. Partner, 'Making up lost time: Writing on the writing of history', *Speculum* 61, no. 1 (1986): 90–117, 94, 05.

16   Bonnie G. Smith, *The Gender of History: Men, women, and historical practice* (Cambridge, MA: Harvard University Press, 1998), 10–11, 104, 266, Note 2. For an argument concerning conversations between literature and science, and feminism and science, see Susan Squier, 'From Omega to Mr. Adam: The importance of literature for feminist science studies', *Science, Technology and Human Values* 24, no. 1 (1999): 132–58.

17   Richard White, *The Middle Ground: Indians, empires, and republics in the Great Lakes region, 1650–1815* (Cambridge: Cambridge University Press, 1991), ix.

9: Character and emotion

1   Thomas Babington Macaulay, 'On History', a review of Henry Neele, *The Romance of History: England*, first published in the *Edinburgh Review* 47: 94, May 1828, 364.

2   Kate Grenville, *Searching for the Secret River* (Melbourne: Text, 2006).

3   Interview with Kate Grenville on ABC Radio National, <http://www.abc.net.au/rn/arts/bwriting/stories/s1414510.htm>

4   Mark McKenna, 'Writing the past', *Australian Financial Review*, 16 December 2005; Inga Clendinnen, *The History Question: Who owns the past?*, Quarterly Essay, issue no. 23 (2006): 16–28.

5   John Hirst, 'How sorry can we be?', in *Sense and Nonsense in Australian History* (Melbourne: Black Inc., 2005), 80–106.

6   Grenville, *Searching for the Secret River*, 185.

7   Grenville, *Searching for the Secret River*, 191.

8   Martha Hodes, *The Sea Captain's Wife: A true story of love, race, and war in the nineteenth century* (New York: W.W. Norton, 2006), 235.

9   Robert Darnton, 'Workers revolt: The great cat massacre of the Rue Saint-Severin', in *The Great Cat Massacre and Other Episodes in French Cultural History* (New York: Vintage Books, 1985).

10   Joan W. Scott, 'The evidence of experience', *Critical Inquiry* 17, no. 4 (Summer 1991): 773–97.

11   Penny Russell, 'A feeling for the subject: feminism, history and emotions', in *Women's History Review* [forthcoming].

12   Darnton, 'Workers revolt', 82.

13   Peter Burke, 'Is there a cultural history of the emotions?', in Penelope Gouk & Helen Hills, eds, *Representing Emotions: New connections in the histories of art, music and medicine* (Aldershot: Ashgate, 2005).

14   Constance Classen, *Worlds of Sense: Exploring the senses in history and across cultures* (London & New York: Routledge, 1993); David Howes, 'Can these dry bones live? An anthropological approach to the history of the senses', *Journal of American History* 95(2) (2008): 119–28; Robert Jutte, *A History of the Senses: From antiquity to cyberspace*, trans. J. Lynn (Cambridge: Polity Press, 2005); Mark M. Smith, *Sensing the Past: Seeing, hearing, smelling, touching, and tasting in history* (Berkeley: University of California Press, 2007).

15   Thomas Babington Macaulay, 'On History', a review of Henry Neele, *The Romance of History: England*, first published in the *Edinburgh Review 47:94*, May 1828, 361.

16   Sigurdur Gylfi Magnusson, *What is Microhistory?* (*History News Network*, 2006 [cited 1 May 2009]); available from <http://hnn.us/articles/23720.html>.

17   Emmanuel Le Roy Ladurie, *Montaillou* (Harmondsworth: Penguin, 1975); Carlo Ginzburg, *The Cheese and the Worms: The cosmos of a sixteenth-century miller*, trans. John & Anne Tedeschi (London: Penguin, 1992 [1976]); Natalie Zemon Davis, *The Return of Martin Guerre* (Cambridge, MA: Harvard University Press, 1983).

18   Ginzburg, *The Cheese and the Worms*, xx.

19   Peter Gay, *Freud for Historians* (New York: Oxford University Press, 1985).

20   David Marr, *Barwick* (Sydney: Allen & Unwin, 1980).

21   Wendy Singer, *Creating Histories: Oral narratives and the politics of history-making* (Delhi: Oxford University Press, 1997).

22 Marcus Rediker, *The Slave Ship: A human history* (New York: Viking, 2007), 344.

23 John Demos, *The Unredeemed Captive: A family story from early America* (Knopf: New York, 1994), 34.

24 Quoting from a letter written on 18 February 1993: Jean R. Freedman, *Whistling in the Dark: Memory and culture in wartime London* (Lexington, KY: University Press of Kentucky, 1999), 88–9.

25 Roy Rosenzweig & David Thelen, *The Presence of the Past: Popular uses of history in American life* (New York: Columbia University Press, 1998); Robert Perks & Alistair Thomson, eds., *The Oral History Reader* (London: Routledge, 1998).

26 Robert F. Jefferson, *Fighting for Hope: African American troops of the 93rd Infantry Division in World War II and postwar America* (Baltimore: Johns Hopkins University Press, 2008), 159–60.

27 E.P. Thompson, *The Making of the English Working Class* (Harmondsworth: Penguin, 1968), 13.

28 Winthrop D. Jordan, *White Over Black: American attitudes toward the Negro 1550–1812* (Baltimore: Penguin, 1969), 582.

10: Footnote fetishism

1 Anthony Grafton, *The Footnote: A curious history* (Boston: Harvard University Press, 1999), viii.

2 <http://www.google.com/search?hl=en&client=safari&rls=en-us&defl=en&q= define:plagiarism&ei=U9QDSrrAGKXm6gPFqISpAw&sa=X&oi=glossary_ definition&ct>; Google, combined definitions of plagiarism, visited on 8 May 09; <http://wordnetweb.princeton.edu/perl/webwn?o2=&o0=1&o7=&o5=&o1 =1&o6=&o4=&o3=&s=plagiarise=>

3 Tony Kevin, *Walking the Camino: A modern pilgrimage to Santiago* (Melbourne: Scribe Publications, 2007).

4 David Hill, *1788: The Brutal Truth of the First Fleet : The biggest single overseas migration the world had ever seen* (Sydney: William Heinemann, 2008).

5 Cassandra Pybus, 'First Fleet follies', *The Australian* (1 October 2008).

6 Anthony Grafton, *The Footnote.*

7 'Statement on Standards of Professional Conduct.' Retrieved 27 April 2009, from <http://www.historians.org/pubs/Free/ProfessionalStandards.cfm>

8 Gertrude Himmelfarb, 'Where have all the footnotes gone?', *New York Times Book Review* (16 June 1991); Simon Schama, 'Clio has a problem', *New York Times Magazine* (29 September 1991).

9   Ann Curthoys & John Docker, 'Is history fiction?', *UTS Review: Cultural Studies and New Writing* 2(1) (May 1996): 12–37.

10 Ann Curthoys, *Freedom Ride: A freedomrider remembers* (Sydney: Allen & Unwin, 2002); Ann Curthoys, 'Freedom Ride: A Freedomrider Remembers: Endnotes to the book.' Retrieved 6 May 2009, from <http://arts.anu.edu.au/history/curthoys/endnotes.htm>.

11 J.H. Hexter, 'The rhetoric of history', *History and Theory* 6(1) 1967: 3–13.

12 Tom Fox, Julia Johns & Sarah Keller, *Cite it Right: The SourceAid Guide to Citation, Research, and Avoiding Plagiarism* (Osterville, Massachusetts: SourceAid, LLC, 2007).

13 Jacques Barzun & Henry F. Graff, *Modern Researcher* (Belmont: Thomson/Wadsworth, 2004).

14 Commonwealth of Australia, *Style Manual: For Authors, Editors and Printers*, 6th edn (Brisbane: John Wiley & Sons, 2002).

11: Tough love

1   Lynne Truss, *Eats Shoots and Leaves: The zero tolerance approach to punctuation* (London: Profile Books, 2003).

2   Patricia Limerick, *The Legacy of Conquest: The unbroken past of the American West* (New York: W.W. Norton & Co., 1988), 105.

3   We thank Alan Atkinson for this example.

Index